Roland B

The Smell of War

Lessons from the Battlefield

The Smell of War © 2018 Roland Bartetzko

Cover by designhouse Prishtina

Contents

Acknowledgements

I would like to express my gratitude to the many people who helped me with this book.

I would like to thank my wife Valbona Mustafa for helping me in the process of editing.

A special thanks to Fiolla Tmava for proofreading and suggestions.

A special thanks to Trim Ibrahimi for formatting and for the cover design and to Faton Kryeziu for his permission to use his painting "Burned Land" for the cover.

Last and not least: Thanks to the soldiers who shared their stories with me so that I could enjoy the privilege to have them in this book.

Part One
Bosnia

A Beginning

"SARAJEVO, Bosnia and Herzegovina, April 19— In an explosion of fighting that appears to have further diminished the prospects of peace in Bosnia, two armies that have been linked in a nominal alliance against the Serbian nationalist forces have opened what amounts to a full-scale war."

-The New York Times, April 20, 1993

"Bitter Croat-Muslim battles in Mostar, sandwiched between cease-fire agreements, will only complicate the already tangled attempts to patch together a peace in the Balkans, Western diplomats in Croatia say."

-The New York Times, May 11, 1993

When I took the bus to the warzone, I was the only passenger. At the time, the city of Mostar was the most dangerous place in Europe and nobody wanted to go there. The bus was old and tattered, seats were missing and there were bullet holes all over the window glasses.

The badly maintained road was winding along the gorges of the Neretva River. When we approached the city, I saw clouds of black smoke rising into the air, long before I noticed any buildings.

The first 'landmark' of Mostar when you approach the city from the South, is the cemetery. When we passed by, I pressed my face against the window to have a better view. I could see that many of the graves were fresh.

When the bus entered the city center, I saw a large graffiti on a wall writing:

WELCOME TO HELL!
MOSTAR, EAST CHICAGO '93

I stepped out of the bus and stood on the pavement not knowing where to go. There were very few people walking on the sidewalk, but suddenly, shooting noise was heard coming from an area a block away and everyone started running.

I stood there alone, not knowing what to do.

A Croatian soldier was waving at me and making an angry face. I told him in German that I couldn't understand a word he said and he shouted in a heavily accented German: "Komm mit, du Trottel" ("Follow me, you idiot!").

As I was running after him feeling a little bit scared and insecure, I couldn't help but notice his strange haircut:

He obviously had been shaving his long black hair when the enemy's small arms fire had surprised him. Now, the left half of his head was cleanly shaven, while the other side was still full of black and dirty hair.

While we were running, he told me that his name was Dragan. I told him my name and why I had come to Bosnia.

We entered a big building, climbed the stairs to the tenth floor (no electrical power) and went into a small apartment. Dragan told me in sign language to lay down on an old couch and have a nap. He would bring me later to his unit.

Of course, I couldn't sleep. It was too hot, too noisy and a million thoughts were crossing my mind. I had come all the way from Germany to volunteer for a foreign military and now that my decision had been made and was quasi-irreversible, I was thinking about my situation:

The Croatian Army wasn't the first army I signed up for. I was only seventeen years old when I joined the German Army. I needed the permission of my parents to do that.

The reason I joined was that I wanted to become a soldier. No more, no less. I wasn't even interested in joining some Special Forces unit. All I desired was to become an infantryman. I joined the German 'Fallschirmjäger' or paratroopers as they were considered to be good infantrymen.

However, the German army was a peacetime army and the chances to see real combat were slim. If it was war you wanted to experience, then the German army wasn't the right place. To call myself a soldier, I thought, I had to fight. Otherwise, I might as well have joined a paintball club.

When the war in Bosnia started, nothing could hold me back from going. I joined the Croats, but I could have easily joined the Bosnian Army, it didn't matter to me. Not the Serbs, though; weren't they the bad guys?

Dragan had left the apartment to go somewhere, but now he was back and told me to go "schnell, schnell" ("fast") with him. We went back to the main road where I had stepped from the bus earlier, and to my surprise, there were three big buses lined up on the other side of the road.

These buses were relatively new, not like the one that I had taken before. We entered the first one and it was full of people and ready to go. The driver wore a military uniform and told us to stand near him during the drive.

The bus left the city the same way I had entered it before, we passed the church and then the cemetery, but then we took a left turn and after about two kilometers, we arrived at the military airport of the city.

The 'Heliodrom' like the Croats called it, was out of use and had seen better days. In the fading sunlight, I recognized the wrecks of some old MIG fighter aircraft that stood left and forgotten on the runway.

We entered the main administration building and I was let into a small office where a group of older soldiers was sitting around a table. They looked like officers to me and it turned out that they were. The most senior of them addressed me. He asked me a couple of quick questions: "Who are you, why are you here, any military experience?" I answered him and that was it. They all seemed satisfied with my answers and each officer shook my hand and congratulated me on my new job. I was now the newest soldier of the Croatian Defense Council.

We went to a small storage depot which was full of uniforms and weapons. I received camouflaged combat fatigues, a pair of US-style army boots, a leather belt, and most importantly, a Russian made AK-47 Kalashnikov assault rifle.

Dragan, who was at my side during the whole time, tried to sneak away with a new uniform for himself, but the guy in charge of the logistics made it clear to him what he thought about shoplifters. Dragan flashed him a smile and while he gave back what wasn't his, I noticed that half his teeth were missing.

I was asked if I knew how to handle the AK-47 and I lied yes. I thought it couldn't be that difficult and I also wanted to give a good first impression. The commander told me that I would get the rest of my equipment at the front line and wished me good luck.

On the Frontline

An old Bordeaux red Renault 18 picked us up and we were driven across the airfield. Then the driver turned off the headlights and hit the gas. We speeded over a very narrow wooden bridge ("Snipers", I was told), turned a sharp left and then stopped in front of a row of bungalows.

Dragan and I got out of the car while the driver immediately turned around and headed back.

In a garden in front of one of the bungalows was a group of soldiers. They were my new squad Dragan told me. A small and chubby guy with a perfectly clean-shaven head and dark bushy eyebrows introduced me to the others. Slaven was his name. He spoke in passable English and after I had shaken everyone's hand, he gave me a quick update on the tactical situation. While he was talking, I could hear the sound of automatic weapons fire. I couldn't say, however, how far away it was, or from which directions the shots were coming and going.

Slaven walked with me through the trenches which connected all of the three single-story houses. We came to the bungalow on the left and greeted a soldier who was manning a machine gun. It was too dark to see anything in front of us, but Slaven told me that the Bosnians, our enemy, had its trenches only about hundred meters away from us. This was the most dangerous place in our defense line, and it was here, where the enemy would most probably attack. We smoked a cigarette and I continued to listen to every word he said.

We were holding a small bridgehead on the Eastern side of the Neretva River and there were constant attacks from the enemy who wanted to get rid of any Croatian presence on the Eastern bank of the river. Only four days earlier, two soldiers of our platoon had been killed by a mortar grenade.

The most important thing to know, however, was that if there would be any trouble, the only way back to safety was the small bridge which I had crossed earlier. "Only at nighttime, though", Slaven told me, "because of the snipers."

I began to understand why I hadn't been under more scrutiny during my 'job interview' at the airport. From a military point of view, this here was a really shitty place to be, and volunteers must have been extremely rare.

It had been a long day and I was getting tired, so Slaven led me into a big cellar under one of the houses. There was a candle burning in one corner and I was told to find myself a place. As it was my first night on the front line, I wasn't scheduled for guard duty and was allowed to rest without interruptions.

Of course, I couldn't sleep for a minute. The mattress I had chosen to sleep on had a putrid smell and I was glad that it was too dark to have a good look at it. I heard some rats rustling in one corner and there were also the cracking noises from small arms fire coming from the outside. I could hear the snoring of a couple of soldiers nearby. I envied them:

They didn't seem to care about the smell and the noise.

Eventually, after lying awake for a few hours, I was too tired to care and fell asleep.

I slowly woke up the next morning, nobody was shooting, the sun was shining from the outside into the cellar and I was thinking: "What a nice morning!" When I slowly began to realize where I was, my next thought was: "Ohhh, fuck!"

For a moment, I regretted my decision to come to this place but then I told myself: "Stop whining and get your ass moving!" and my moment of regret was over.

I was determined to learn as much as possible during the next weeks to make it out alive!

During the next days, I quickly picked up the 'secrets of the trade'. Although I had been a paratrooper in the German army, I realized that I had a lot to learn.

I immediately started learning the new language. We were in the middle of a war and I knew that my life could depend on my language skills. It wasn't only about understanding the orders given to you on the battlefield, but also to know what's going on in general, the tactical situation.

I had a small notebook and wrote down the most important words and phrases: The numbers, directions, military terms, but also how to order a beer and to compliment people on their cooking skills (the next days, I would get invited a lot for lunches and dinners). What you learn in a textbook from school is very different from what a combat soldier needs to know, and so my list looked really strange and it included a lot of swear words.

I also had to improve my infantry fighting skills. I slowly figured out which of the things that I had learned in the German military were useful and which weren't.

Most important, however, were my instincts. I had to develop a sixth sense to detect the danger. I needed to know what sound a bullet made when it passed close to my head, the places where the enemy might have placed an anti-personnel mine and what the signs of an imminent enemy attack were.

Instincts come with experience. I figured out that if I would survive the first month, I would have a much better chance to make it through the war alive.

Observations

Here is some advice for every new soldier on the front line to make things easier:

Be a little coward! Take it easy in the beginning and don't volunteer for any dangerous assignments. Wear your body protection, even when the whole squad is laughing at you.

If you have dreamed of becoming a war hero, receiving a medal or being a great patriot fighting for your country, your first day in a combat zone is a very good day to bury all those dreams.

From now on, your only aim is survival. Don't try to play the cool guy! You are the rookie and you better listen to the advice of your more experienced veterans.

Learn and adapt fast! To do that you must ask questions. You will get on everyone's nerves, but there is no other way to do it.

Think for yourself! Not everything you have learned in basic training is applicable in combat, but, on the other hand, not all the advice that comes from your more experienced squad members is golden either.

Therefore, you can't just trust blindly all the advice given to you, but you have to sort out which procedures and tactics are the best in your situation.

Always be aware of the situation! Listen carefully to every briefing. At the beginning, you might feel like you are the least important squad member and all you have to do is just to walk behind the rest of the team, but you need to know what's going on, where you are, where you are going and what the enemy is up to.

Always be careful! After a while in combat, people become negligent. They do not follow safety and security procedures like they should do, because "everything always went well".

Negligence, however, is one of the worst killers on the battlefield.

The first days and weeks are the most dangerous for a new soldier. After you have been through them and have adapted to your new environment, your chances to survive will become much better.

The City

After a couple of weeks in the trenches, I began to explore life behind the frontline. On my first excursion, I went with two guys from my unit to a bar near the airport. The bar was packed, there was no place to sit and we barely found a spot where we could stand. I thought we would never get served and told my friends that we should leave, but then one of them addressed the crowd:

"Shut up everybody! This guy here with me is German and he came here to fight for your stupid asses!"

In no more than ten seconds, I found myself sitting at a table with my friends and there were at least five bottles of beer in front of me. More and more were coming from the bar. Somebody ordered food and the party started.

My second trip brought me to Medjugorje which is a Catholic pilgrimage site in Bosnia. My staunch catholic brothers-in-arms insisted that I should go there with them. While they prayed inside the cathedral, I waited outside and kept an eye on our automatic weapons.

Even during the war, there were a lot of pilgrims visiting who came from all over the world. On my second or third trip there, I met a young Italian woman who had been living in the city for a couple of months. She was convinced that the devil had taken possession of the whole city and its inhabitants and that it was her mission to fight against it.

Every time I went to the city (which was not far from the airport) she would show up out of nowhere and it was very hard to get rid of her. She spun endless stories of her fight against evil and how she got herself kicked out of almost every hotel and bar. I didn't mind: I wasn't a fan of the local population either; they didn't like us because, with our uniforms and weapons, we scared the pilgrims away. Aside from her weird streaks, this Italian lady was a nice person.

One day she was gone, just like that. I had a lot of things on my mind at the time and couldn't look out for her, but I would sometimes wonder what might have happened.

Many times I was invited to have lunch or dinner with a Croatian family. It would have been very rude and out of the question to refuse such an invitation. Sometimes, I had no choice but had to eat two or three lunches a day!

Therefore, one of the first words that I've learned in the Croatian language was 'dosta!', which means "enough!" Sharing your food with a stranger was an especially kind gesture as most civilians were poor and barely had enough food for themselves.

A new problem presented itself to me. Because of the heat (it was July) and the lack of water, I had been unable to have a bath or a shower. I began, first to smell and then to stink.

I was once again invited for dinner at a Croatian family's home and sitting on a couch, waiting for dinner to be served, when I realized how badly I was smelling. My army T-shirt which had once been olive green had more of a blackish color now. It had a putrid, rancid, almost rotten smell which slowly found its way into my nostrils.

To make matters worse, two young women came into the room, the house owner's daughters I presumed, and they sat down on the same couch and started a conversation with me. I was very embarrassed and studied their faces, waiting for them to react to my body odors.

Nothing happened. They must have taken at least a whiff, but they didn't show it. Obviously, they were used to bad smells and, to be honest, the city didn't smell much better than the front line.

I learned that our body odors aren't really a problem on the battlefield. Somebody is trying to kill you and this is not a good time to be fastidious. There are hundreds of things that smell worse and nobody cares anyway.

By far, the worst smells were those of rotting bodies. Sometimes people got shot in places where it was too dangerous to retrieve their corpse. Then they started decomposing and an extremely disgusting and sickening sweet smell filled the air. There weren't only human bodies, but also animals, often cows, horses, and dogs that had stepped on the anti-personnel mines in front of our positions and died.

Observations

Taking care of your hygiene isn't an easy task when you are in a warzone without enough water and no electricity. There are three body parts that you must keep clean, even on the battlefield. If one of those parts gets infected or causes you any other trouble, the war will be over for you:

Your teeth. I always had a toothbrush with me. I used the plastic bags from the combat rations to protect the brush from dirt. You get used to cleaning your teeth while doing something else at the same time (like watching the terrain, listening to an officer giving orders or checking your rifle). There is really no excuse for not brushing your teeth.

Your butt. You can use wet wipes to wipe your ass. If you don't have any, try to clean your butt (and your genitals as well) with water from time to time. You should also change your underwear whenever you can. There is always some space in your backpack to take some spare underwear with you.

Your feet. Always carry at least one pair of spare socks with you! Change your socks whenever there is an opportunity and let the old pair dry. Wet wipes or alcohol are perfect for cleaning your feet if you have no water.

Sometimes, if the situation allows for it, just take off your boots for a few minutes to let your feet get some fresh air.

You will get quickly used to this 'field hygiene', but sometimes, you will be tired and just want to rest and then you really have to push yourself to make this extra effort and dedicate a minute of your time for your personal hygiene.

If you follow this advice and keep these three body parts clean, you will be fine!

The Parrot

Meanwhile, I had lost sight of my old friend Dragan but managed to replace him with an equally strange person. My new acquaintance, whose name was Goran, was also a soldier in our platoon. He was only nineteen years old and he was one of the 'cowboys':

A typical cowboy was about nineteen or twenty years old and had already spent two years in the army. These guys practically went from the classroom to the front line. Too young to worry about any possible consequences, not married and no children, they simply didn't give a fuck. They were thriving!

In civil life they were nobody and now overnight they had become heroes.

Of course, these cowboy types were damaged goods. My buddy Goran was a complete alcoholic. As I was about to learn, he also was a thief:

One evening, he decided to go into the no man's land between the frontlines to look if there is anything valuable in the abandoned apartments there. As he liked to drink a lot, he was probably searching for some alcohol.

He dressed up in civil clothes and went into the night. We didn't hear from him until the next morning when the Croatian Military Police brought him back to us.

He told us that in the beginning, everything went fine. When he arrived at the frontline, he told the Croats there that he will go to his flat in the no man's land (A blatant lie!) to pick up some of his mother's stuff (Another lie). The Croats revere their mothers and therefore, the Croatian soldiers let him pass through their lines. He told them that he would be back in no time (His third lie.)

While he was rummaging through the abandoned flats, he found a bottle of wine and started drinking. With the bottle in one hand, he continued his 'mission'. Suddenly, he heard some noises coming from a flat. Someone was shouting for his wife: "Ženo! Ženo!" ("Woman!"). Maybe an old man, having been forgotten there - and all alone?

Our comrade didn't hesitate and entered the place from where the voice came. There was no electrical power, so he used a cigarette lighter to help him see in the dark. The flat was empty and no old man was inside. Then from behind the couch, the voice sounded again: "Ženo!" Our friend took a look and there it was: A big cage with a green and blue feathered parrot inside, curiously mustering the intruder.

Goran found a towel, put it over the cage and took the bird with him. In one hand the cage and in the other hand the bottle he returned towards the Croatian lines. Unfortunately, he somehow had forgotten which road to take and turned up at another section of the frontline.

The Croatian soldiers on guard duty shouted at him to stop and a searchlight was turned on and pointed at him. From the distance, our friend must have looked quite suspicious. He was told to stop right there and not to move. Two soldiers approached him, weapons ready and pointed at him. Our man told the two soldiers that he was a Croatian soldier and so they asked for his military ID card.

The ID was in the back pocket of his jeans and to reach it he put the cage on the ground picked the ID and showed it to the soldiers.

The Croats started to look surprised and as he looked at his own hand he saw that it wasn't his ID, but a pocket calculator that was in his palm. He had found the calculator in one of the flats, but had totally forgotten where he had put it. At the same moment, the parrot started screaming again.

The Croats were convinced that they were dealing with a crazy person. Therefore, they brought him to the next Military Police station, where luckily somebody knew him (It was not the first time that he ended up there) and brought him back to our unit.

Observations

Our friend was very lucky not to get shot as he made almost every mistake possible while approaching a group of soldiers.

Here are some tips how to do it right:

Don't move at night. Soldiers tend to be more scared and trigger happy at night times. If possible wait until sunlight before moving around.

Don't wear military style or very dark clothing. You might be mistaken for the enemy.

It's always better to approach a checkpoint on foot than by car. If you have a car, stop a hundred meters before the checkpoint and then walk up there.

It's good to have a white flag with you. Even a white handkerchief on a stick will do.

Don't hold any objects in your hands.

If there are other people around, get close to the kids and stay away from male adults. Everyone likes kids.

If you speak the soldiers' language then start shouting as soon as they are close enough to hear you: "Don't shoot! I'm a … (Name of the group of the population they are not eager to kill.)

When you are close enough, offer them cigarettes! Cigarettes are the ultimate peacemaking device.

You can start some small talk, but choose the topic wisely.

If necessary, bribe them. Bribing is a form of art, so be discreet! Don't let everybody see that you have money. You can put some money bills between the pages of your passport; if they check your passport they'll take the money. This is the most common form of checkpoint corruption.

If you have no money, cigarettes will do just fine.

Don't act as if you are scared. Be self-confident, but don't exaggerate!

It's good to get your story straight when you are being interrogated. So make up your mind before they tell you to talk. It is important not to arouse suspicion or curiosity. Tell them what they want to hear.

"Where are you from?" and "Where are you going?" are the top two checkpoint questions. If you can answer them correctly (not necessarily truthfully), you should be fine.

Snipers!

I soon learned that the biggest threat, not only to the soldiers on the frontline but also to the civilians in the city, were the snipers. Every daily activity was influenced by them: Where to go and where not, where to sleep and eat, when to run and when to take cover.

In Mostar, the frontline ran through the middle of the city so that almost every place in town was within the reach of sniper fire.

When I visited Croatian families at their homes, the first thing they told me was which side of the apartment was the 'bad side' where you couldn't go near a window or stay on the balcony, "because of the snipers."

Every car that entered the city went full speed through the streets to avoid to get hit. Still, this was the safest method to move from one place to another.

On one occasion, a soldier of our platoon didn't want to wait for the old Renault, tried his luck by foot and was shot while crossing the small bridge. He got half of his genitals shot off and when I visited him in the hospital a few days later, he was still in excruciating pain. This incident served as a warning to all of us.

I cannot recount how many times I was shot at by a sniper. The first few times, I was quite scared, the bullets would make a nasty sound when they had just missed my head or struck a wall nearby, but after a while, I got used to it.

One afternoon, we were drinking coffee in our garden in front of our bungalow when a sniper took aim at us. We didn't even stop drinking our coffee until the fourth or fifth shot nearly missed us. Only when a bullet hit our platoon leader's coffee cup did we decide to abandon our activity and take cover.

Sometimes, we were able to strike back at them. Some guys from our brigade identified an enemy sniper on the top of a ten-story building. They were able to enter the building undetected and made it to the top floor. However, when the enemy sniper saw them on the roof he decided to jump from the building.

Luckily the enemy's snipers were not very accurate. Their first shot almost always missed and that gave us ample time to run for cover.

Sometimes, they didn't even really try to hit us or maybe we were out of their reach and they were just shooting at us to make our life as unpleasant as possible. They definitely had succeeded.

Observations

The best way to survive when a sniper is shooting at you is to make a run to get out of sight. A sniper can't shoot very accurately at a fast moving target and in most cases, you'll be fine.

Don't run for cover! If you are attacked by a machine gun or small arms, it makes a lot of sense to run for cover, but not during a sniper attack. Machine gun fire can hit you when you are running and even when the shooter can't see you; they just shoot hundreds of bullets in your direction and hope that one will kill you. Therefore you need to have a good cover.

A sniper, on the other hand, wouldn't waste his ammo on an invisible target. Even when you are hidden behind a 'wall' of blankets or laundry (or smoke!) which is easily penetrable by any kind of sniper ammo, no sniper would waste a single round on you.

To run out of sight, however, is tricky. Often, you don't know exactly from where the sniper is shooting which makes it difficult to determine the enemy's line of fire. In Bosnia, we would usually run around the next corner of a building and then get inside. If there are no buildings, you can run into some bushes or, if everything else fails, you hide behind a car.

In case you want to go after the sniper, there are the two basic elements you need to know: Detect and destroy.

Detection is half of your job. Once detected, snipers can be neutralized or forced to withdraw. Several things can give you a clue from where the sniper is shooting:

The muzzle flash often gives the sniper's position away. There are devices that will suppress the muzzle flash and/or the sound, but they often limit a sniper rifle's performance

It's very hard to identify a sniper's location by the sound of the gun. Still, it can give you a general direction.

Sometimes the reflection of sunlight on the sniper's scope might give his position away. This won't be the case, however, if your adversary is a specially trained professional.

Ideally, you have observers with binoculars and night vision devices in your unit who are permanently looking out for snipers and can direct you.

A good way to locate an enemy sniper is to ask your own snipers. The number of possible sniper positions is limited and your own snipers will have a good guess where the enemy might be.

After you have spent a while on the battlefield, you will get an eye for possible sniper positions. We usually scanned the roofs when fighting in an urban area. Enemy snipers would often remove a shingle and shoot at us from there. So if you saw a house roof with one or two missing shingles you were immediately alerted. In Mostar, snipers were often positioned either at the top of larger buildings or they were hiding inside an apartment and removed a couple of bricks from its wall to have a good shooting position.

Once the sniper is identified you direct your fire at him. The more the better. Mortars and heavy machine guns are especially effective. The best countermeasure against snipers, however, is your own sniper fire.

Sometimes this is not enough and you might want to go after the sniper with a group of your own infantry. To do this you use basic infantry tactics and common sense. There is no 'special tactic' for hunting snipers.

If the sniper has a free field of fire in front of him you can use fog or smoke grenades to disturb his vision. Especially in urban environments, your success will depend on the intelligence that you possess. If you are aware of the sniper's exfiltration route you might be able to cut him off. You might also be successful if you are able to locate the sniper's alternative position(s) and either await him there or mine them with booby traps.

Still, a specially trained sniper is not easy to catch. When dealing with enemy snipers you have to be prepared and aware of them before they start shooting at you. Protect yourself, your positions and your movements, always bearing in mind the 'sniper threat'.

Baptism of Fire

Life on the frontline slowly became a routine for me and I had turned from a rookie into an apprentice. I experienced getting shot at a couple of times, mostly sniper fire, but on one occasion I merely dodged an RPG (Rocket Propelled Grenade).

It was a very hot summer that year and we grew tired of sleeping in the stickiness of our cellar. The first guys started to sleep in the bungalows and more and more of us followed their example. This was reckless! The enemy had a few pieces of heavy artillery which could easily penetrate the roofs of our houses and the cellar was much safer.

The last time my unit had suffered a heavy artillery attack was a week before my arrival. Two soldiers had been killed then, but this was now more than a month ago and one month is an eternity in war.

There wasn't enough place in the house so some of us even slept in the garden. One morning, we were awoken by a heavy explosion coming from the garden. An RPG rocket had exploded behind the well. Seconds later, more grenades were incoming and the enemy also started shooting with machine guns. We were all expecting an attack and everyone grabbed their guns and their chest webbings and we ran into the trenches near the house for cover.

Nothing happened, though. After a while, the Bosnians stopped shooting and a couple of minutes later, we were back in the house, drinking our 'kava' (Turkish coffee) and eating breakfast.

A couple of days later, we had some important visitors:

A reconnaissance unit from Croatia came to our bridgehead and started to observe the territory with some big binoculars. The next day some high ranking officers arrived and were discussing their plans over maps and aerial photos.

This was part of the preparations for a major offensive. The Bosnian Croats had assembled thousands of troops, about half their army, to make a decisive attack against the positions of the Bosnian army. Our unit was right in the middle.

Preparations had already started many days before, but nobody told us that there would be an attack. It wasn't necessary, we saw the signs everywhere.

Two days before day zero, a mortar unit set up a dozen of 82 mm mortars in our backyard. And finally, when there was only one day to go, a complete mechanized infantry brigade from Croatia arrived. As my unit was our brigade's intervention unit, the freshly arrived Croats sent their own intervention unit to join us. We would attack together with them.

It was all very busy and crowded at our camp during these days. People coming and going. Trucks bringing ammunition and weapons.

Finally, all preparations came to an end and the support and logistics troops left us in the afternoon. Dusk settled in and everybody knew that the next morning would be the day. Some alcohol was served and we were reminded not to drink too much of it. One of my comrades didn't listen and passed out somewhere. Another one started vomiting, not from the alcohol, but from stress and anxiety.

Most soldiers were busy preparing their gear, cleaning their rifles and getting ammo for their guns.

Around midnight, a blue cotton ribbon was given to each soldier. We were told to put them on our uniforms to easily recognize each other as friendly troops. This was necessary as our enemy had very similar uniforms to ours.

After midnight an eerie quiet settled in. All weapons were cleaned, checked and double checked. Everybody was prepared and there was nothing left to do than wait. You can clean your weapon only that many times and puke your guts out only once.

In these last moments, most soldiers preferred not to talk to each other, but to stay for themselves. I saw some of them praying. Others tried to sleep, but most of us were just laying down on our flak jackets, staring holes into the night sky and smoking one cigarette after another.

This moment reminded me of all the soldiers and armies in history who found themselves in the same situation. From ancient Germanic tribes, the French in Dien Bien Phu to our own enemy who was just a couple of hundred meters away. They must have felt the same thing. Being part of a big army going into combat you feel big and tiny at the same time. Fate is out of your hands and you can just hope and pray that tomorrow at the same time you will still be alive. You look around and watch your comrades. To see how they cope and to remember their faces. Some of them won't come back.

My friend and squad leader Slaven interrupted my thinking. We were called to pick up our gear and to advance to our starting positions. As our base was practically in the center of the attack, we just had to sit there and watch the other units leave, wondering what will happen to them.

Then came our turn. We walked a few meters to our trenches to await the final signal for the attack from there. It was now absolutely quiet and dark. No talk, no cigarettes. Everybody's eyes were directed towards enemy territory.

Then a small *'blob'* sound behind us, seconds later a sound over our heads, like a gush of wind or a swarm of wild geese flying over us and finally a big explosion in front of us, right in the middle of the enemy's positions.

The waiting was over and the game was on.

Attack!

We left the trench in small groups of five or six soldiers. I was the last soldier to get out. This was my first 'big' battle and I was told to take it easy which was fine with me. We were walking in single file, because the first soldier had to keep us clear of the mines. We had mined the whole area around our base just a couple of weeks earlier and although nobody had made any maps that could show us where the mines were, the guy we had put to walk in front had a good memory and knew which places to avoid.

Our own artillery now started a massive barrage. As we advanced so did our artillery fire, constantly hitting targets about two or three hundred meters in front of us.

After about two hundred meters we came to the first buildings of an enemy village. There was nobody there. We had expected some resistance, but not a single shot was fired at us. There were not even the unavoidable dogs around to bark at us. The village was totally dead, so we thought. We slowly passed through it and nothing happened.

Behind the village were several railroad tracks. We were about to enter a big industrial area. In the upcoming light of dawn, I could make out warehouses, an oil refinery with several huge oil storage tanks and a lot of smaller buildings, like pump stations and office buildings. There were plenty of railroad tracks going in every direction and on them were dozens of railroad wagons of all kinds.

While we navigated ourselves towards the oil refinery, a bullet zipped over our heads. Used to getting shot at, we continued our way without even looking up. After a minute a second bullet hit a nearby railway wagon. The more we approached the refinery the more shots were fired at us. They seemed to be coming from all directions, even from the village that we had left behind. Every time a bullet hit a railway car, it was ricocheting from the metal surface with a nasty 'pling' sound. From somewhere somebody with a megaphone started yelling: "Allahu Akbar!"

We ran the last meters to the refinery. The bullets were now raining upon us. We hunkered down in a trench near a giant oil storage tank which luckily seemed to be empty. Every time a bullet hit this storage tank it resonated like a drum. Soon it was like a thousand drums were playing all at once.

Now the first enemy grenades were hitting nearby. Mortar and RPG grenades, which could be fired only from a close distance. Although by now we had complete daylight, we still couldn't figure out from where the enemy was shooting at us. We encountered another small group from our unit nearby. They had made out an enemy position at the far end of the refinery and decided to attack it. I saw one of the guys fixing his bayonet to his AK rifle. Then they disappeared. We also decided to move, but in another direction, one towards a big warehouse building next to the refinery.

The building was half empty and we used its cover to take a break from the bullets and grenades, smoke a cigarette and wait for orders coming over the radio. This was a warehouse from a tea factory: There were thousands of teabags everywhere around us: Chamomile tea. The smell of it soon became intolerable.

By listening to the radio communication we got a clearer image of what was going on: Obviously, there were still enemy troops in the village we had marched through earlier on. They either hadn't seen us when we sneaked through or they had decided to let us pass. Either way, the enemy was now between us and our base. They were in well-camouflaged positions and we were an easy target for them. Furthermore, the group of soldiers we had encountered earlier on near the refinery was now in serious trouble and had suffered its first casualties.

We were ordered to retreat. Now we just had to find a way back. We decided to try our luck by following the railway line in one direction to get around the enemy village and then to cut through open ground and reach our own lines. This was easier said than done: We left the warehouse on the opposite side from where we've entered it and met two more groups of our unit. It seemed that by retreating from the enemy's fire most of our unit had ended up right in this spot. We all took cover in a long trench which ran along the side of the building.

Snipers were now starting to aim at us while mortar and RPG grenades were hitting the trench. It was clear that if we would stay there any longer we would all be doomed.

The only way out was a small road, but there was absolutely no cover for at least 400 meters. We started to leave the trench in small groups of two or three while the remaining soldiers shot cover fire.

I was in the last group to leave. When I jumped out of the trench I ran over the first dead body just a couple of feet away. I ran maybe ten meters before I fell to the ground and started crawling. There were bullets everywhere. A friend of mine crawled just in front of me and I saw how some tracer bullets were hitting the tarmac just inches away from him. Another soldier behind me got hit in the leg and started screaming.

We managed to crawl down the road until we were stopped by a big wire fence. It was too high to climb over it: All the soldiers who escaped the trench were piled up in front of this fence and were attracting enemy fire.

Finally, we managed to cut through the wire of the fence by connecting an AK bayonet with its scabbard. This makes a perfect wire cutter. On the other side of the fence, we continued crawling.

About a hundred meters further down the road, I reached the first of our own defense positions. I entered a small bunker, its floor was covered in blood. A wounded Croatian soldier was getting first aid there.

Meanwhile one of our Croatian T-55 tanks was approaching from behind us to cover our retreat. Under its protection, we started to evacuate some of the wounded soldiers along the road.

One by one, our soldiers returned from the battlefield, but after half an hour, there were still many of them missing. It started to dawn on us that many of the missing wouldn't come back at all. One guy in our group was anxiously waiting for his brother who was fighting with another platoon.

I saw two soldiers going over to this guy and talk to him. I couldn't hear anything, because of all the noise around us, but when I saw that our soldier started crying, I understood what must have happened. Slaven came over to me and confirmed what I already knew:"He lost his brother."

There was nothing I could do for him. I was called back to the battlefield to evacuate the wounded and I felt almost relieved that I could do something useful and didn't have to witness my buddy's misery.

The enemy artillery started to direct their fire at us and we had to go for cover between two empty buildings. There was an older soldier there, standing all by himself. I remembered him from the day I arrived at the airport. We had smoked a cigarette together, but this seemed a long time ago. He was some kind of officer, had spoken a little German with me and had teased me a little bit, but in a friendly way.

Now he was all alone and didn't talk. He was crying. He had lost his son.

It was utterly disturbing to watch this grown man break down. These guys were supposed to be the backbone of the army's morale and seeing him cry was the ultimate sign that all had gone to shit. One of the soldiers took him by the hand, almost as if he was a child, and led him back to safety.

The Aftermath

In the evening we took count: From the eighteen soldiers in our platoon, six were killed on that day and another two were missing. The next day we learned that they also got killed. The guy that I saw planting his bayonet on his AK was also dead. One of our snipers was heavily injured by a shot in the head and died later in a hospital.

The week after the battle was filled with funerals. These were very sad affairs: most soldiers who were killed were very young, almost kids, and it was heartbreaking to see their parents' despair.

The saddest thing, however, happened near the end of this 'funeral week'. The comrade who had lost his brother in battle got killed when an artillery shell hit the car he was driving. Another soldier who was with him in the car also died.

During their funeral, we came under heavy artillery fire, but luckily nobody got injured.

After the 'funeral week', the Croatian army had decided to send the surviving rest of us to a holiday at the seaside. I spent my time there sitting on the beach, getting drunk, and dreading the day when we had to return to the frontline.

On Sleep

You are extremely tired, but in a few hours you have to attack the enemy and you are scared for your life. How do you get some sleep? Sleep deprivation is a serious problem on the battlefield. When it accumulates, it will affect your performance and you will become less alert and make more mistakes. Every mistake on the battlefield, however, can be fatal.

The only way to overcome sleep deprivation is to sleep. Even in a combat situation, most soldiers will adapt and find some rest. Here are some tips:

Sleep alone. The army likes to have everyone at the same place, so when they issue orders they don't have to look for each and every one. This, however, is not helpful when you are trying to sleep. I often sneaked away from the pack on the frontline and made my own little place a couple of meters away. Everybody knew where I was 'hiding out' in case something important happened. This way I got far more sleep than I would have gotten in an overcrowded and stinky shelter.

If you are not able to seclude yourself physically then try at least to create the illusion of it: stick earplugs or earphones in your ears, wear sunglasses or 'disappear' under a blanket.

Cover. You will sleep much better when you are covered in a blanket or a poncho liner. If it's too hot, take off your shirt, but cover yourself.

Hats and caps. You will sleep easier with a hat on. Look at the cowboys! Especially at daytime, the brim of a hat will give you (the illusion of) privacy and darkness.

Use every minute! Often you are told that there will be only a "five-minute break" and you might think that this is not enough time for a nap-you are wrong. Usually, these five-minute breaks stretch and stretch and become twenty minutes or half hour breaks. You'll regret that you haven't tried to sleep in the first place.

If necessary, set an alarm. You'll sleep better if you know that something or someone will wake you up, because you don't have to worry about oversleeping.

Most importantly:

Don't give a crap! I was always the guy who slept a few meters away, while everyone else had such 'important' things to do like analyzing the situation, worrying about their girlfriends at home or what will happen tomorrow. If you want to get some sleep you must be able to let your mind go blank and to leave all your worries for later.

Don't be squeamish, either. In a trench, under a vehicle or on the back of a driving tank, any place will do. "You can't sleep there!" doesn't exist.

Not Again!

SARAJEVO, Bosnia and Herzegovina, Sept. 19— Forces of the Muslim-led Government Army advanced against Croatian militiamen in central Bosnia and near Mostar today in intense fighting despite a cease-fire that was supposed to have taken effect on Saturday, local news reports said.

-The New York Times, September 20, 1993

Back at the frontline, nothing serious happened for the next couple of weeks and I started to relax a little. I thought that maybe the first attack which had ended in disaster had just been an exception and that the rest of the war would be a little less intense.

A couple of days later, however, a military jeep turned up at our position and a bunch of officers jumped out of it, carrying bags with documents and making very serious faces. I knew immediately that something was up. I looked at my comrades and I saw that they were worried, too.

The officers disappeared into a nearby house together with Tomo, our platoon commander, while we were waiting for them to come outside and tell us what was going on. These were some of the longest minutes of my life. These officers didn't show up on the front-line to drink coffee; that much was clear.

After half an hour, Tomo was the first one to emerge from the house. When I saw the concerned expression on his face, I knew things were bad. He carried a number of red colored cotton cloths in his hands and I felt like someone had punched me with a fist in my stomach! These cotton cloths were like the blue ones that we had received before the last battle. They were used to recognize friend from foe and were only issued before a major offensive operation.

I was convinced that if this new mission would go as badly as the last one, I would probably not make it out alive.

I felt sick, doomed and utterly hopeless.

Only less than an hour ago, I had thought that the war would be an interesting adventure, sometimes dangerous but now I had figured out that it was exactly the other way around: Mostly dangerous and only sometimes interesting.

There was nothing we could do. Orders had to be followed, even if it would mean your death. Each of us attached a red cloth to his uniform and then the waiting game started: We were counting the minutes until we would attack.

After another hour, a call over the radio informed us that the attack had been cancelled, at least for the moment. None of us felt relieved, though. We knew that this operation was just postponed and that sooner or later we had to go back into combat. The waiting game wasn't over.

Observations

I was exhausted, although I hadn't done any physical work. The fear was eating me up and I knew that I had to come up with something very quickly. Every time you go into battle, you are scared shitless. The panic will rise inside of you and you have to develop a technique to keep it down. The trick is to keep your fears under control:

First, you have to know your fears. There are several kinds of fear a combat soldier has to deal with:

First of all, there is a 'deployment or mission fear'. This starts the day when you get your orders to go into combat. It's like a fist in the stomach. From this day on, until you come back home to safety you will feel this fear. Sometimes it's just a gloomy feeling, the certainty that you are doomed and sometimes, it makes you wake up in the morning with thoughts like: "Fuck! What have I done?!"

This fear is the easiest to control. Keep busy, avoid moments of loneliness and stay focused on the task at hand. Fortunately, as soon as a soldier gets his or her marching orders, life becomes very busy and there isn't much time to start with deep thinking, anyway.

The second fear is the 'battlefield fear'. This is the concrete, clear and present fear in face of a life-threatening situation: To get shot, to get maimed by a grenade or to step on a mine. Every soldier has a different method to manage this fear:

I used to lie to myself that the situation was much better than it looked; that the enemy wasn't that close, the shots were not aimed at me and the sound behind the bush was an animal and not an enemy soldier.

My auto-suggestion method worked out fine for me. I also invented 'mantras' to calm myself down. One of them went like:

"Today is a good day to die. But not for me. Not today!"

Of course, endlessly repeating that you are not dying today, won't increase your chances to survive, but you can fool yourself into believing that it does.

It worked and I calmed down.

Other soldiers were using other methods, a lot of them were praying, others sang songs and some soldiers overcame their fear through shouting out loud or cursing. I lied to myself or repeated my mantras. Whatever works for you is fine.

The third type of fear, however, is the worst. It's not only related to combat, but all of us will experience it one day. It's the fear of imminent death. That you won't be there anymore. In combat, this happens when you are in a really hopeless situation.

This fear is the worst feeling I have ever experienced, almost like if somebody pushes you from a cliff and you have only seconds to live. You feel completely alone.

In the end, there is nothing you can do to overcome this fear. While other fears can be managed, you cannot train or prepare for your last moment on earth.

New Friends

It had been now five months since I had joined the war and it was time to look back and take stock:

The number of rounds shot in the enemy's direction: Maybe fifteen rounds which make half a magazine. The number of times the enemy shot at me and tried to kill me: Dozens of times with thousands of bullets, plus some RPGs and a few times where I couldn't figure out what had hit us.

I had heard about a unit consisting solely of foreigners that was operating in a nearby region and decided to check it out. I took the bus to Čaplijina, only about thirty kilometers away from Mostar, went into their barracks, asked them if I can join and was accepted immediately. This went even quicker than my first job interview at the airport. I wasn't the greenhorn from Germany anymore but someone who had seen the battles around Mostar and its airport. By now, I enjoyed a certain respect in the army.

This so-called 'foreigner platoon', or 'stranci vod', in Croatian, was part of a bigger Croatian brigade which was commanded by a Croatian Colonel who had served ten years in the French Foreign Legion.

Obviously, he had had the plan to open up his own Foreign Legion, but somehow it didn't grow bigger than the size of a platoon. Most foreigners were Germans, but there were also people from the Czech Republic, Hungary, France and many other nations. Our platoon leader was James, a Brit who had served in the Foreign Legion's famous parachute regiment.

I had no problems in adapting. I spoke English and French and my Croatian had also become quite passable, so I was able to talk to almost anyone in my new team.

Our duty schedule was almost boring. We would spend two weeks on the front line and then one week in a reserve position and another week on holiday. Enemy activity was very low and if it weren't for the few artillery shells that came down on our positions once or twice a day, one might have thought that we were participating in a maneuver.

Our enemies were the Serbs now. The Croats had made a peace deal with the Bosnians who now became our Allies. Some hardcore Croatian nationalists in our brigade didn't seem to like it, but our leaders were professional soldiers and orders had to be respected. While some soldiers complained, others took the opportunity and went on their free week to the Bosnian side, mostly out of curiosity, but some of them visited their old friends from high school who, because of faith and politics, had become our enemies for a while.

The best thing about my new outfit was that we were getting paid! It wasn't much, but when you are three weeks of the month on the front line and have only one week left to spend your money, even a small amount is enough.

I went to see the coast of Dalmatia, some islands in the Adriatic Sea, but my most preferred destination was a small bookshop in the town of Split that sold used books in English. Whenever I had time, I went there and bought a book. I would take books with me on the front line and to my big surprise, I wasn't the only one.

The English speaking soldiers of our unit liked to read a novel series called 'Vietnam-Ground Zero'. A good read when you sit in a trench waiting for something to happen.

This went so far that we started to use Vietnam era call signs, acronyms and terms in our daily life, like "klicks" instead of kilometers and other stuff.

Our French-speaking comrades preferred to read the soft porn-pulp-secret agent novels from Gerard de Villiers, called 'SAS'. Not exactly the cream of French literature.

I read Henry Miller's 'Tropic of cancer' and 'Tropic of Capricorn' which I adored. I also read many books written by Umberto Eco and Laurens van der Post. If you are fed up and tired of war, these books help you to take your mind off.

On the front line, you read books to pass the time, but not to figure out what combat is like. No need for books here: All you ever wanted to know about combat, you are about to learn in practice.

Life would have almost been good if it weren't for some small problems. There was this Italian guy in our unit that I really couldn't stand. Stefano was a short, but very muscular dark haired Sicilian ("I'm Sicilian, not Italian!") who was boasting all the time, lacked discipline and also was, in my opinion, a lousy soldier. To make matters worse, he was a squad leader in our platoon and liked to order me around.

The day came when I became a squad leader myself and I could see the look of disapproval on his face.

One day in late September, we found ourselves on the top of a hill when his squad came under enemy fire. My own squad was to his left and I had a good look at what was going on. The firefight took only five minutes and then everything calmed down, except for sporadic sniper fire.

Suddenly, I saw Stefano walking up to me. I was thinking: "What the fuck does he want?" He approached me with the most neutral expression on his face and with a matter of fact voice he stated: "I just shat my pants. You don't have any wet wipes with you, by coincidence?"

Too surprised to come up with some smart ass remark, I just said: "Sure, there you go!" and gave him some baby wipes. He immediately started cleaning the droppings out of his pants, just in front of me!

I was flabbergasted! This guy really didn't seem to care much about his misfortune. I wondered why, from all possible solutions, had he come to ask me? There must have been enough soldiers in his own squad who could have helped him out. Plus, I was almost his nemesis, so what was his motivation?

I didn't have to think long before it dawned on me: Stefano was the squad leader and it wouldn't help his authority if he had asked one of his own soldiers. Additionally, he needed a spot to clean himself up away from his men. He had no choice, but had to take the risk and cross the sniper fire to come to my position.

He could be sure that I wouldn't tell anyone. It would have been considered very bad etiquette if I would have started telling people about his accident. I was a squad leader just like him and you were supposed to stick together, even if you didn't like each other.

I couldn't help it, but had to admire his thinking. Very logical. And then, of course, there was the way he had approached me: if there would be a "what to do when you crapped your pants-for dummies" book, then this was textbook behavior! He behaved as if he had only spilled a cup of coffee over his uniform and it must have cost him a lot of effort and acting skills to go through with it. I had to admit it: he had handled himself very well.

After this incident, we got along much better. I had come to realize that this guy indeed had some good qualities. It seems like sometimes, you have to shit your pants to show the world what a guy you are!

Scary Times

While in Mostar, every day had been a fight for life or death, here in Central Bosnia, things were going much easier. However, not unlike during my time at the airport, when you get a little bit bored and complacent, shit is going to happen.

Soon, we were sent to a forested area on the crest of a hill where our enemy, the Bosnian Serbs, was only a few hundred meters in front of us.

During the day we could see them walking around in their trenches, always busy working on something. We also had our trenches and we were taking turns: Two guys on trench duty, while the rest would stay behind in a little hut about a kilometer away.

One afternoon, we received a message from our Military Intelligence guys telling us an attack against our positions was imminent. So we did our best to prepare, checked our weapons and got more ammo.

At around 22:00 it was my time to leave our hut and walk up to the crest to man a position in the trench. Usually, we would go there in pairs, but I always preferred to go there alone: It gives you time to think and you are less distracted.

On this night there was no moon, constant rain, and a lot of wind. At around midnight a battle started at my right flank where our Bosnian allies were positioned. I could only see some faint lightning. At first, I wasn't even sure that what I was seeing was a battle and not a thunderstorm. James, my platoon commander, came up in the trench and briefly explained the situation to me.

I wasn't really worried: The Serbs had obviously decided to attack our neighbors and not us; this was perfectly fine with me.

As the night went on, the rain and wind stopped and a thick fog came and covered everything. I couldn't see a thing, not even my own hands. I just stood there in the trench and tried to stare holes into the fog.

After a while, I heard some noises in front of me. Somebody was approaching my position, but I wasn't sure if it was an animal or the enemy. The sound faded, it was calm again, but when I almost thought that the whole thing had just been a product of my imagination, the noises came back. I could distinguish voices, very faint, but clearly, there were human voices.

I knew that somewhere near me we had a machine gun in place and I slowly paced my way to find it. As I couldn't see anything, I put my hand on the edge of the trench and felt my way along the edge until I touched something metallic.

I checked the weapon: It was loaded, and I just had to remove the safety. My hands were shaking and it took me forever to switch the machine gun to fire mode.

Finally, I was ready. I just had to wait for the enemy to come up the hill. I was worried that the Serbs would just bypass me and continue their way to our hut and even further, but there was nothing I could do. Any moment I expected the shadow of an enemy soldier to appear right in front of me.

I heard more sounds: Several pairs of boots marching in the grass and some voices, all very near. I opened fire, three short bursts in the direction of the voices.

Now my ears were ringing from the sound of my shooting and my eyes were blinded by the muzzle flashes of my gun. I was deaf and blind and alone on that crest and somewhere out there in the foggy night, there was a group of people who were trying to kill me.

After what seemed like an eternity to me, two guys from my unit arrived and asked me what had happened. I told them and we conducted a quick check of the vicinity to see if I had hit anybody. As the weather was getting worse again, we soon abandoned our search and my fellow comrades left me and went back to our shelter.

I had another hour to stay in the trench before two soldiers of my unit came up and released me.

The next morning we heard that a neighboring Croatian unit had come under fire. Their commander came to see us and we figured out what had happened during the night: Due to the bad weather, the Croats on our left side had missed the way to their positions and went straight into enemy territory. When they realized their mistake they turned around, missed another road and showed up right in front of my position where they came under my fire. Thankfully, nobody was hurt.

Although I went through many situations which were much more dangerous than this one, I've never been so freaked out. Alone on that hill, blind and deaf, the (supposed) enemy somewhere near; that really gave me the creeps. It was an almost surreal experience.

Observations

After a year in the war zones, I wasn't the same person I had been before. Every combat soldier goes through this process. Starting from the first day of the war, a soldier's personality starts to change. You can divide this 'transformation to become battle-hardened' into different stages:

The 'New Guy'

Fresh recruits arriving in a battle zone are often pumped up and seem full of self-confidence. I've seen nineteen year old kids trying to tell me what to do on their first day in the field. The new ones think they know it all and only a few of them are willing to listen to the old "farts". In reality, these fresh soldiers feel very insecure and their boasting is a way for them to hide their fear and anxiety from their comrades. This phase is the shortest of all phases, sometimes it lasts less than a full day in battle. In the case of our nineteen year old new comrade, it lasted less than two hours. After I got wounded in battle I went to see a medic far behind the frontline and there was the new guy, huddling on the side of the road, completely paralyzed by fear.

The 'Baptized', or the 'Apprentice'

After a short while the new guy shuts up and either he gets to business, or he goes home. Having received his baptism of fire, he or she starts to develop all the necessary skills to survive on the battlefield which can't be taught in training. This phase lasts a couple of weeks, all depends on the intensity of combat. The 'apprentice' is not yet a fully trusted member of the unit and therefore mostly charged with secondary tasks, for example as the second man on the machine gun. Nevertheless, they get the job done and are well respected.

The 'Fighter', or the 'Battle-Hardened'

After weeks in combat, many soldiers have honed their skills and have acquired survival instincts. They 'smell' where a shell will hit, where and when the enemy will attack or which position to choose. They don't panic. This 'fighter' feels comfortable around his fellow fighters with whom he forms a brotherhood. These guys don't like to talk much and you'll rarely see them laughing. Somehow the horrors of combat have deprived them from most of their human emotions. They are the 'battle-hardened' who form the backbone of every combat unit.

The 'Battle Weary'

If a fighter stays in combat for too long, his skills will deteriorate. While the 'fighter' is fearless, but careful, the 'battle weary' often avoids combat. He has seen many of his fellow fighters die or getting wounded. Most probably he has also been injured more than once. Although desensitized to the maximum, you can't suppress human emotions forever and eventually, PTSD will take a toll on you. These soldiers usually have severe drug or alcohol abuse issues. While the 'fighters' are already not the greatest talkers, the 'battle weary' barely talk at all. I've seen some of these guys in Bosnia and it always struck me how passive they were.

Don't get me wrong: They were great guys and very friendly and they deserve our greatest respect. But unfortunately, they are also completely unfit for battle and therefore a well-functioning military organization needs to carefully monitor their combat soldiers and retire individuals as soon as they show the first symptoms of battle weariness.

Prisoners

I had come back to our barracks after a weekend on the Adriatic coast and met with my buddies in the chow hall. There was a soldier sitting all by himself who got my attention. He didn't talk to anybody, didn't touch his food and I saw that one of his ears was missing. Later on, one of my comrades told me his story:

This Croatian soldier was fighting in a dense forest when a bullet hit his leg. Separated from his unit he was captured by the enemy. Although wounded and bleeding he was severely beaten up. Then the enemy dragged him to the next Serb city where a mob of civilians was already waiting for him. They wanted to burn him alive and just when they got a big fire started and were ready to throw him into it, the military police showed up and saved our man.

He was then put on the back of a truck and brought to Banja Luka, which was the capital of the Bosnian Serbs. During the drive, more prisoners of war were thrown into the truck at every stop, where they were all beaten with rifle butts and iron rods. When the truck finally arrived at its destination, half of the prisoners had died.

The captured soldier then came to a military prison where the beating went on. The Serbs mistakenly thought that he was a brigade commander, so he got interrogated and beaten even more. Finally, they realized that he wasn't the big fish they expected him to be and he was somehow treated a little better, but he still got beaten up at least once a day.

The Croats negotiated his release and after a couple of months and after paying a 30,000 dollar for 'lawyer fees', he was released. Being a tall guy and a former boxer he was down to only forty-five kilos and had lost one ear and all his teeth.

We also had a guy in our company who had been taken prisoner by the Bosnians. He was taking five showers a day and was washing his hands every five minutes. During his time as a Prisoner of War (POW), he had never been allowed to clean himself up and was now overcompensating for it.

I would get a little taste of life in prison myself. It was summer and although this was usually the time with the heaviest fighting, there wasn't much going on, and I got pretty bored.

One night, I had a drink with my platoon commander, the former French Foreign Legion paratrooper. He told me that there was a mixed Bosnian-Croat unit fighting in Central Bosnia that was always looking for volunteers. I was immediately interested and decided to go there and check it out.

This was much easier said than done. To reach my new unit I had to travel through large parts of Bosnia, a country ravaged by war where nobody exactly knew where the frontlines were or what was going on. My platoon leader himself had been severely beaten up, robbed and almost killed when he made the trip himself two years before.

I started early in the morning and took a bus to Tuzla, the most Northern Bosnian city. Although the Croats and Bosnians had stopped fighting each other and had formed a confederation against the Serbs, there was still an atmosphere of hate and distrust between them. I had to be careful: The Bosnians might hate me because I had fought against them earlier, and some extremists Croats might consider me a traitor, because I wanted to volunteer for a mixed Croatian-Bosnian unit.

Everything went surprisingly smoothly. I reached Tuzla in the late afternoon. I found a cheap hotel room and decided to stay overnight. I would rest and try to catch a ride north the next morning.

What I didn't know (and nobody else did, either) was that on the very same day, forty miles to the East, the Serbs had started their final push against Srebrenica and a large number of refugees was coming our way, blocking every road North and East of Tuzla.

The next day, it soon became clear that there was no way for me to go further north, at least for a couple of days. I didn't want to stay in Tuzla either and took a bus to a Croatian enclave a few kilometers to the South. I was confident that I could wait out the Serbian offensive there and try my luck again a couple of days later.

At the first checkpoint of the Croatian enclave, I was ordered out of the bus and brought to a Military Police station. I didn't speak Croatian very well and therefore a woman who had lived in Germany was called to translate for me. I was interrogated for about half an hour ("What you are doing up here, where are you going" ...) and the police didn't like my answers. They had never heard of any foreign volunteers that were fighting for the Croats and I was therefore immediately under suspicion. They told me that I would be detained for a maximum of three days, and meanwhile, the police would check out my story.

I was then put in a jeep by two military policemen and brought to a small military complex in another part of the small city. This complex turned out to be their POW camp. There was a single-story building which housed about eighty prisoners in twelve rooms. I was brought to a small room where I found three prisoners lying on their bunks. Two of them were Bosnian Prisoners of War and one was a Croat who was in for murder.

I already knew from other parts of Bosnia that it never made any difference for which reason a person was detained; all prisoners were always put together and treated the same. A comrade in my unit once had spent three weeks in a POW camp in Croatia (he had sold his assault rifle) and was kept with Serbian POWs in one block: being imprisoned with Bosnian POWs came as no surprise to me.

I found out that all rooms housed about four to six prisoners, except for one big room which had more than ten prisoners. In this bigger room were a group of Mujahedeen from a number of Arab countries that had volunteered to fight for the Bosnian army.

It was mid-July and extremely hot. My room had only a very small window which didn't allow for much air to circulate. Outside of the window was a German shepherd dog that immediately started barking every time someone came near the window and tried to look outside.

There was no electricity. In the evening we got a candle, but there was nothing interesting to see anyway so this candle was good for nothing.

Only one toilet for all prisoners. If you needed to go you had to knock at the door, call your room number to a guard and then wait. This could take sometimes three or four hours. As soon as you were in the toilet, the guard who accompanied you would already tell you to hurry up as there were always other prisoners waiting. The toilet was just a hole in the floor and there was a shower head just above it. Once in every ten days, you were allowed to take a cold shower, standing above the shithole.

There was no possibility to shave and I soon grew a beard. To do our laundry we were allowed to take a bucket of water into our room and somehow wash away the sweat from our clothes.

Food was scarce and each day it was the same: Breakfast was a slice of ham with more fat than meat and tough like chewing gum. For lunch, the guards put a very large cooking pot filled with water over an open fire in the yard. Then they would simply throw in some canned food and warm it up. The problem was that the tins were under a lot of pressure and when you opened them you had to be very careful:

Once I found some soap that somebody had left in the toilet and took a bucket of water to clean my T-shirt. I let it dry, happily put it on (my first

49

clean shirt in weeks!), opened a can of beans and got half of its content spilled all over my shirt.

In the evening we always got a small tin of liverwurst and sometimes some sardines. There were simply not enough calories in our meals and although I didn't move around that much, I rapidly lost weight. Some prisoners were allowed to work outside and they sometimes brought some additional food with them which was always welcome.

Surprisingly, I wasn't searched when I entered the complex and I still had my wallet with me. The only thing we were allowed to buy was cigarettes, so I would give a guard some money and he would come back after a while with the smokes. This went very well and I don't know how I would have made it without the cigarettes.

There wasn't anything to do. Aside from the heat, the terrible hygienic conditions and the lack of food, boredom was our worst enemy. After a while, you knew all the stories of your fellow prisoners and they started repeating themselves. There were no books and no newspapers. We had a small radio, but it was wartime and there were only radio stations that played patriotic songs or spread a lot of propaganda which was getting on my nerves: better no radio at all.

Each day we were allowed to spend half an hour in the yard. A small area had been surrounded by barbed wire and a soldier with an assault rifle was watching while we made our rounds.

During my stay, I never saw more than two or three guards at the same time. On the daytime shift, there was a young one who was quite friendly and an older one with no teeth who was incredibly stupid and always tried to provoke me. He would start with things like:

"While you are rotting away here, your comrades on the frontline are in a heavy battle. I heard it on the news last night that your brigade has lost a lot of people!"

This talk really made me angry. I couldn't hide my anger and it showed on my face which made the guard enjoy himself even more which then resulted in me getting even angrier. This guy somehow knew how to push my buttons, I had to admit that. Maybe he wasn't that stupid after all.

I didn't see anyone abusing prisoners, but sometimes at night, a couple of soldiers would enter the room where the Arabs were staying and then we could hear their screams. I once met one of the Arabs on my way to the yard and had a little chat with him. He came from Jordan and has been a student before he joined the 'Mujahedeen battalion' of the Bosnian army. He had been a POW for almost two years, but he seemed to be in good spirits.

The Mujahedeen in this camp were all caught in uniforms and while the Bosnian POWs were allowed to keep their uniforms or wear civilian clothes, these guys had to wear the ugliest kind of tracksuits I've ever seen. They were pastel-colored and obviously the leftovers from a Red Cross humanitarian clothes donation. Bad enough to be a POW, but imagine running around the whole time in a pink-colored tracksuit!

The more time passed by, the more I grew concerned about my own fate. In the beginning, I was told that I would have to stay only for a couple of days, but now I learned that there were prisoners who had been told the same thing and they were in for months!

I started talking and complaining to every guard that I could see and after a couple of days some higher up in the military police learned about my case and ordered my immediate release. I said goodbye to my fellow prisoners, gave a fake smile to the toothless guard (who looked really pissed off) and was put again in a jeep, this time to be driven back to my old unit.

I arrived at my old unit in the late afternoon and when my comrades saw me, they all started laughing. I had grown a beard, my clothes were totally dirty and somehow this seemed to amuse them.

I took a long shower and went with three of my buddies to the next town to a pizza place. I ate for two and drank a couple of beers. My friends updated me on what had happened during the last weeks and told me that there were reports of a large number of missing persons in the area where I had traveled. There were also rumors that a lot of civilians had been murdered by the advancing Serbian forces, but nobody knew for sure.

I felt very glad that I had come out of this experience alive and relatively well, but I felt that this trip might have left me with some psychological wounds which could haunt me in the future.

Many things happened that were as intense as my time in the POW camp and I almost forgot about it. Still, during some quiet moments, I sometimes remembered those days and wondered what had happened to the other prisoners in the camp.

Observations

I hope that no one will come into such a situation, but if you do, here are the things to do when you got captured:

Prepare yourself! First of all, during a combat mission, don't carry anything on you that could potentially harm you when getting caught. This means not only military information, but family pictures, home addresses and everything else that makes you vulnerable.

Tattoos that are depicting unit emblems, political or religious symbols might also get you in a lot of trouble. 'Semper Fi', 'Kill them all- let god sort them out' or 'I love Jesus' might not go down so well with the Taliban. These tattoos might even haunt you years later. A lot of Croats who live in Bosnia still have to cover up their 'Ustaša' tattoos when traveling across the country, even years after the war. A Swedish volunteer who served with me in Bosnia got stabbed by some Bosnian refugees in his Swedish hometown after they found out that he was fighting against their people.

The first hours after being taken POW are critical. This is the most dangerous time as you are often in the hands of trigger-happy combat soldiers pumped with adrenaline. They might just kill you for one false move.

Those first hours are also the best opportunity for you to escape! Combat units are not trained to guard POWs and often they don't have enough soldiers to spare to properly secure their prisoners. Later on, you will have to deal with military police or specialized units which will make an escape much harder. Further, if you decide to escape from a military prison or an insurgent camp your enemy will retaliate and kill your comrades that you have left there.

Don't expect a special POW status. In modern conflicts which are often counterinsurgencies, the Geneva conventions for the treatment of prisoners of war do not apply. You might be banged up with common criminals or civilian hostages. Therefore:

Most of the 'informal' prison rules are also valid for POWs. For example: Mind your own business. Avoid eye contact with other prisoners and guards, but especially:

Don't trust anybody! You might have some cell mates you don't know. They might be spies to hear you out or simply try to take advantage of you for their own survival.

During interrogations, don't think that you can outsmart your opponent. And don't play dumb! Most of today's regular and irregular armies have sophisticated intelligence organizations. You will deal with professionals who know what they are doing. As there is probably not much what they don't already know, there is also no reason to play the hero: Spill the beans and tell them what they want to know. Forget the "Name, Rank and Unit" thing.

Even after having provided them with the information you might get beaten up, raped and tortured just for the pleasure of your captors. They enjoy hearing you scream in pain. There isn't much that you can do, but some POWs succeeded in pretending that they had passed out. Then the torturers usually gave the victims a break to recover.

After the torture and interrogations there will be extended periods of boredom and isolation. Try to keep your mind busy by remembering events, books and movies, songs or prayers.

Never give up hope! You might be saved much sooner than you expect.

Try to take care of your body! Most probably you won't have enough calories in your food to allow you to do much sport but try at least to keep your body flexible with some stretching.

Use every opportunity there is to clean yourself, especially your teeth, your feet and your behind.

You might get sentenced to death or to a long prison term for 'war crimes'. This is most often a bluff and serves to destroy your morals. If your captors have kept you alive for that long you will probably have more value for them alive than dead.

Your biggest problem will be to stay mentally fit. There isn't much you can do against the physical torture anyway.

What you do after your release is also very important. Don't hesitate to ask for psychological help. Often the family of a former POW plays an important role in his recovery. It's important to have somebody to listen to your story.

Don't think you can shake this off easily. Aside from being killed, being a POW is the worst thing that can happen to you in a war. You might feel mentally strong after your release, but the problems will come sooner or later, sometimes after months or years.

Having been a Prisoner of War will change a person completely. Accept that you are not the person you were used to be, but somebody different and explain this to your loved ones.

Big Operations

"PARIS, Sept. 15— As the Serbs fall back in disarray, a Greater Croatia is taking shape in Bosnia and the likelihood is growing that Croatia may emerge as the real victor of the wars of Yugoslavia's destruction.

Since Sept. 9, when their offensive began, the Croats have swept across a wide area of western Bosnia, taking Drvar, Sipovo and the strategically crucial town of Jajce.

The attack has involved at least three brigades of the Croatian Army as well as Bosnian Croat forces, military analysts said."

-The New York Times, September 16, 1995

I almost missed the last big offensive of the Bosnian war. I had spent a weekend on the seaside to get away a little bit from the rowdy pack and when I came back to the barracks, I found them empty. A handwritten letter from James, our platoon commander, was lying on my pillow which read:

"Hey! Get your ass to our forward operation base and report to the brigade ASAP!"

That was all. I packed my stuff in seconds and took a cab to the next city. Then I hitchhiked until I reached the last civilian village before you entered the warzone. I was in luck, a jeep from my brigade passed by. I hopped in and they drove me straight to a location in the forest where my brigade had held a position for the last weeks.

When I came to our trenches, however, they were all empty. The brigade was moving quicker than I did and I grew more and more frustrated. Just when I sat down on my backpack and started thinking what to do next, I heard the noise from another jeep. It was an old Nissan from my platoon with Stefano, our Sicilian-Italian volunteer on the wheel! I still didn't like him, but at this moment, I was really glad to see him.

He drove very fast and at the same time gave me a quick update on the situation. Our unit had been alarmed early in the morning and was forming the spearhead of a new offensive operation.

My platoon was further ahead and was mounted on two of our old T-55 tanks. The enemy was in full retreat and nowhere to be seen. A couple of minutes later, we were out of the forest and I could see an army convoy ahead of us, led by the two tanks.

I got out of the jeep and ran to the first tank. James sat near the gun and greeted me. There was no place for me on this tank so I had to climb on the second one.

Two Croatian soldiers with mine detection equipment were in front of the convoy. As they were on foot, we advanced very slowly. Our mission was to reconnoiter an area at the left flank of our brigade and then rejoin with the main body of our attack force.

We were almost finished with the mission and were only about two hundred meters away from our own positions, when the mine detection crew took off their headsets and went to one of the jeeps behind us. They had obviously thought that their job was done.

The driver of the first tank floored the pedal and his tank went full speed ahead for the last two hundred meters. The rest of us just watched them disappear behind a cloud of dust. Just before they reached the friendly territory, there was a big black cloud. Then we heard a loud boom and we saw human bodies falling from the tank in every direction. The tank had hit an anti-tank mine!

We immediately ran to help them. James had gotten several inches of metal shrapnel through his right foot. I saw a big chunk of metal protruding out of his army boot. He asked us for a morphine injection, but none of us had any. Then, after a minute, we could see how the pain kicked in. He had been a French Foreign Legion paratrooper and he bravely fought what must have been an excruciating and agonizing pain.

Tears shot out of his eyes and he started to swear a lot, but he didn't shout or scream. After five minutes, a medic arrived, and our man finally got his injection. His pain was so intense that they had to give him another shot, just a few minutes after the first one.

Then I saw another guy sitting nearby on the ground. There was no blood on him and therefore we all assumed that he was alright.

Later on, however, we learned that the blast of the mine had completely destroyed his eardrums and had also messed up his balance which is located in the inner ear. He had problems in determining where was up and down and often fell out of his bed or from a chair. The army sent him to a hospital where he had undergone several surgical procedures, but he unfortunately never managed to recover. Worse still, he developed some serious mental health problems.

That evening, we were back at our base in a small city. The army tended to keep everything secret and therefore, a lot of speculations and rumors would pass around about what was going to happen. We weren't too depressed that our platoon leader was taken out; most of us were far too busy to prepare themselves for the upcoming action and simply had no time to think about the fate of their unfortunate comrade.

Pierre, a Frenchman, had taken over the platoon. He was an amiable and funny man who happened to look more like a Catholic priest than a warrior, but you learned quickly not to misjudge him. He was small, a little bit too fat and wore a pair of small round glasses which made his eyes look like buttons. I couldn't understand him when he talked English in his heavy French accent but then again neither could anybody else. We liked him.

We were woken up at four o'clock in the morning and this time, our company got on a bus. During the drive, we could see a number of villages burning in the dark. We went deeper and deeper into what was considered enemy territory only a couple of hours ago and we were surprised how far the enemy had retreated. Finally, after two hours of driving, the bus stopped and after a short briefing, we again climbed on a pair of old T-55 tanks that were leading a column of military vehicles.

It was now early morning and it promised to be a sunny day in mid-September.

The column started with me sitting behind the turret of the second tank. I enjoyed the fresh morning air and the drive. For me, riding on a tank was fun! I had a very heavy load to carry and was extremely glad for every single meter that I didn't have to walk.

After only a kilometer, however, we were told to dismount as we were approaching the enemy's positions. Obviously, our commanders had learned something from our last tank ride. Another platoon of our company took the lead while we were marching behind them.

Our battalion's recon element, which was far ahead of our column, got under enemy fire and was cut off from the battalion. Our company commander who was with them got shot in the leg. Pierre came towards me and ordered me and our machine gunner to go forward and check out the situation. We checked our equipment and left our comrades.

The road we were advancing on lead through a canyon, on the left bank of a river. While we were moving forward, the enemy was shooting at us from above, as well as from the front. As I continued my way, a couple of artillery shells hit a few soldiers in front of me and caused a panic. I almost got trampled down to death by the retreating soldiers. I shouted at them but to no avail.

Finally, we found our lost comrades, brought our machine gun in position and covered the retrieval of the wounded soldier.

As we looked for a good position for our machine gun, we found an empty house and climbed the stairs to the upper floor. There was a big window of which we broke the glass in order to be able to shoot. There was a dense forest in front of us. After a while, I heard noises coming from of the woods: The enemy was approaching!

I took a grenade from my vest, straightened the pin at its end and placed the grenade on the windowsill. I continued to hold my rifle, but if I needed to use the grenade, it was just in front of my eyes and ready.

I heard someone moving through the forest, took my gun and pulled the trigger. Nothing happened! My weapon, a Hungarian made AK-47, was jammed!

I immediately did the drill routine, checked the magazine, reloaded, tried again-nothing! Meanwhile, our Recon element was gone and in safety and we were left alone to confront the enemy. I changed the magazine, tried again and this time everything worked fine. So it was the magazine.

I remember thinking to myself that this was the first time in my life that my weapon jammed while in combat and it could not have come at a worse moment. A very shitty feeling. Everybody is always telling you that the only thing in war that you can really rely on is your weapon and then this happens!

When it was our time to leave, we came under heavy machine gun fire. As there was nobody there to cover our retreat, the enemy had all the time to take good aim at us. One bullet hit my shoulder and I fell down on the road. I touched my shoulder and felt the blood. The enemy continued to shoot at us and the only way out was the river. So we jumped into the river and swam about a kilometer back. There we found a house where several Croat soldiers had taken cover. They gave me first aid and I continued the way back to my unit. After I rejoined my platoon I was driven to a hospital to be given necessary care.

The interesting part began when I was on my way to the hospital. The driver of the ambulance had an American made M-16 assault rifle with him which he showed me with no small amount of pride.

We started driving and after a few kilometers, a deer was crossing our path. As my wound was not life-threatening, the ambulance driver and the medic who was with him asked me if I would mind if they go for a little hunting. I didn't and the guys left the car to shoot the deer. It was a small one and it fit easily into the back of the ambulance.

About two hours later we reached the hospital. The doctor who examined my wound told me that I was extremely lucky as the bullet had just missed an artery. While he attended my wound, somebody put a bottle of beer in my hand and I started drinking. Before I was ready to go, I drank another bottle. The medical personnel then told me that it would be best if I stayed a couple of days in the hospital just to make sure that there were no complications or infections.

I declined the offer and decided to go back to the front line. Although I wasn't fit to fight, at least for the next couple of days, I decided to stay as close as possible to my unit. The war in Bosnia was in its decisive phase and sometimes units were sent far away from their home bases and stayed deployed for months. I didn't want to wait out the rest of the war in the Bosnian 'hinterland' and so I better went right away.

Over the next few days, my shoulder got stiff and I couldn't move my arm without feeling immense pain. I then realized that I was very lucky. I've seen a guy get hit by a pistol bullet in his stomach and he almost died. He spent months in a coma and years later on he still had serious health problems.

I rejoined my platoon in a small city that had just been taken from the enemy. When my comrades saw me, they all had a surprised look on their face. They heard that I was hit by a bullet and thought they wouldn't see me for the next few months. We found a house where we could sleep and I lied down on a couch and read a few pages of a paperback that I had brought with me: 'Thus, spoke Zarathustra', from Friedrich Nietzsche. What better place to read it?

The next morning we were told that we were going on a so-called 'cleaning operation'. This meant that we had to go into the mountains to search and destroy enemy elements which might have been cut off from their main force and might pose a threat to our logistics and support troops.

Our enemy was in retreat and we were ordered to catch up with them and cause as much damage as possible. This was extremely risky as we had no time for a careful advance. The whole time while we were slowly moving through the dense forest, our officers complained to us over the radio that we were too far behind. The rest of our brigade was advancing on paved roads and was already miles ahead of us.

To make things worse, it started to rain. After two days and two nights of marching up and down the wooded hills of central Bosnia, we were completely exhausted. My duty was to protect our rear, so I had a good look at my fellow soldiers marching in front of me. After a while, I saw that one of them had started swaying from side to side, almost like a drunk man. I asked him what's going on, but he didn't reply.

Half an hour later the guy suddenly stopped and said: "I can't go further, I'm dead!" We all halted and Pierre, my squad leader, came to assess the situation. We decided to take his backpack and that everyone would carry some of his gear.

We were already carrying a lot of weight, but now each of us had to take another ten pounds. The only thing our exhausted comrade still had on his person was his assault rifle and two spare mags.

This whole 'weight redistribution' exercise had cost us more minutes of precious time that we didn't have. Therefore, we had to walk now even faster, we were almost running. This went on for a while, but after another hour, it was clear that this guy couldn't move on.

We couldn't leave him behind either so it was decided that another two soldiers would stay with him and that they would return all the way back to join our support troops.

Our enemies were now far ahead of us and our chances of catching up with them were getting slimmer and slimmer. Our platoon's combat strength were three men down and so we were split into two elements. This mission was turning into a complete fiasco, only because of one man's insufficient physical fitness.

To make matters worse, I had begun to develop the symptoms of a severe case of diarrhea. Thinking that it couldn't possibly get any worse for me, Pierre commanded me to walk point! This meant that I had to walk as the first in our formation, always facing the danger of getting shot at or ambushed.

There was no way to refuse the order and say: "I'm sorry, but I got the shits!" Each one of us had his own personal problems: Pierre had just returned from the hospital himself after he had been shot in the leg and I saw that he was still limping a little bit. Still, he didn't complain. I said to myself: "Clench your teeth and deal with it!"

I quickly went to our medic and asked him if he had some charcoal tablets, but he said that he hadn't.

On the next day, it continued raining and the rain didn't stop until the end of our mission. We were in a hurry more than ever.

At every break we made, I ran to the next bush or tree and emptied my bowels. I didn't care if anyone was watching or what they might think: I felt terrible! Cold sweat ran down my face, my stomach cramped and I was already feeling exhausted after marching the first kilometers.

At the same time, I was walking point and was on the lookout for the enemy. It was the constant tension and adrenaline flow that saved me from shitting my pants: As long as I was scared or excited, I didn't feel my stomach cramps or the need to relieve my bowels. However, as soon as there was a calm moment, even if it was only one minute, I had to rush to the next bush. I had just come back from another 'session' when our medic saw me and asked what was wrong.

I said: "I got the shits! What do you think why I asked you for the charcoal tablets?" To my bewilderment, he replied: "That's what you wanted them for? Well, I don't have those tablets, but I got some other medicine to treat diarrhea…"

I snatched the pills he offered me out of his hands, swallowed them dry and soon felt much better. My diarrhea was cured, but my stomach was completely empty now. We carried almost nothing to eat with us and I was getting hungry. The enemy was gone and all we had to do was to descend the mountains and make contact with the rest of our brigade.

We were all at the end of our forces when we finally hit a tarmac road. A couple of hundred meters further down the road, two trucks from our brigade were waiting for us. Hungry, tired and miserable as we were, these two trucks were the most wonderful thing we had ever seen!

The Badass

We were driven back to our starting point in the city and rested there for the next two days. Then we were brought to a small village called Majdan where we spent a week guarding the new frontline. The villagers were all Croats and in the beginning, they were quite happy to see us. They invited us to their homes and while we tasted their homemade 'rakia' (booze), they told us horror stories about what they had gone through during the Serb occupation.

We almost began to feel like proud liberators, but after a couple of days, the villagers seemed to get tired of our presence. Many of our soldiers were drunk all the time and if it wasn't their chanting that kept the villagers from a good night's sleep, then it was our heavy artillery that was positioned in a field near the village.

After a week without events, we were once again on the offensive. This time, there were no buses to drive us, nor were there any tanks, but once again, we had to walk over the hills and mountains.

After a day's march, we had reached a small wooden hill when we heard an engine's noise coming out of the forest in front of us.

One of our comrades came running to us and shouted:"Tanks!" I started watching the expressions on all my comrades' faces, ranging from surprise to panic.

Then I saw this tall Croatian soldier: Totally relaxed and with a smile, he only shrugged and said: "So what?"

We made our RPGs ready, but the enemy didn't advance further. After the situation cleared (we got the order not to engage) I went to see this guy. I wasn't the only one: His cool demeanor hadn't gone unnoticed and there were two other guys with me who wanted to know more.

When we found him, he was sitting in the grass, smoking a cigarette. We grilled him until he told us his story:

About a year ago his platoon was defending a small village in the middle of nowhere, far away from the next friendly unit. One night, he went to sleep there, but was abruptly woken up the next morning:

"My bed was shaking. I first thought that it must be an earthquake, but after a while, I realized that it couldn't be. I heard the sound of motors, got up and went to the window. When I removed the blinds and opened it I saw what had been causing the shaking: A whole convoy of enemy tanks was passing by, right under my nose."

The previous night our soldier had decided not to sleep where all his comrades were sleeping, but to find himself a nice bed in one of the many abandoned houses in the village. Early the next morning the enemy had started to advance and his buddies, totally outnumbered, decided for a hastily retreat. In the ensuing commotion, they didn't realize that they were one man short.

Our comrade continued:

"There was no sign of my unit and I realized that they must have been gone without me. One enemy soldier who passed by looked up at me and nodded: He must have thought that I was one of them. I got away from the window and for a moment a wave of panic swiped over me. Then I put myself together and started thinking: If I would panic, I would die for sure. So I told myself to be calm and to start thinking."

Our friend continued his escape story: He forced himself to wait out for the night and then started walking across the village. There were enemy soldiers on almost every corner, some of them talking to him. The most difficult thing was to control his voice when replying to them. Fortunately, none of the enemy's soldiers suspected anything and they all thought he was one of them. At the end of the village, he slipped through the enemy perimeter and then it was done. He just had to walk for the rest of the night to reach his own lines.

This night had a lasting impact on our friend:

"After this event, I decided that there was nothing in life that could freak me out anymore. Every time I find myself in a dangerous situation, I compare it to this night and tell myself: "If you could stay cool there, then there is no reason to lose it now!"

Obviously, his 'system' worked. We were all deeply impressed. Definitely badass!

We were told to stay on the hill and prepare to defend it. As long as nobody attacked us, there wasn't anything to do and so we sat on the grass, smoked cigarettes and watched what was going on in the valley down below us.

Three Croatian brigades had engaged two enemy brigades and the fighting took place just alongside a small road that went through the valley, just in front of our eyes. For the rest of the day, there was just a lot of noise and smoke. We watched the whole battle from a relatively safe distance, almost as if watching a war movie.

We didn't know it yet, but this was the last big battle of the Bosnian war. Two weeks later, we were told that there was a ceasefire and that we were not allowed to shoot anymore. We thought: "Yeah right!" as this wasn't the first time someone told us about a new ceasefire only to see it broken after two or three days.

Our commander seemed to grasp what we were all thinking and he said: "Don't you guys laugh! This time it's for real!"

At the end of the year, my unit was sent to a small village on the frontline and our job was to guard a road that led straight to the enemy's positions. The problem was that there was no road: it had completely disappeared under masses of snow.

As we knew that our enemy wouldn't attack us with all the snow, we all went into one of the empty houses of the village and tried to stay warm.

For two weeks, it didn't stop snowing and we were stuck. The army couldn't send us supplies and after a couple of days, we were roaming through the empty houses to find something to eat. There was a small sled and with it, we carried the wooden furniture from the other houses to use as firewood. Walking around became an almost impossible task.

We stayed inside, everyone huddled around a small fireplace in the kitchen and we started rationing our cigarettes. We had totally forgotten that there was an enemy outside and I'm sure that our enemy also didn't waste a single thought on us.

During extreme weather conditions, nature becomes your first enemy. You are too busy surviving nature to have time to care about your human enemy. In any case, the war doesn't go anywhere and there will always be time to fight another day.

After two weeks, the snow stopped, a bulldozer cleared the road and the army sent a truck with another unit to relieve us from our outpost. We had been completely isolated, but now the truck driver brought us the latest news:

A peace deal had been brokered. The Croat side had to give back all the territories that we had conquered during the last offensive, our soldiers had to move back to barracks and we were told to start looking for a job. The war was over.

Part Two
Kosovo

Another Beginning

"The long-simmering tensions in Serbia›s province of Kosovo turned violent in recent weeks and threaten to ignite a wider war in the Balkans. Only a concerted diplomatic effort by the United States can keep the conflict from escalating."

-The New York Times, May 10, 1998

While in Bosnia reigned peace, a new war in Europe was making the headlines. I was sitting in a bar in Southern France reading a newspaper when I stumbled over a small article on one of the last pages:

"Has the Kosovo Liberation Army lost the war?"

I was intrigued. I knew for a long time that there was unrest in this tiny Serbian province, but I never heard that the Albanians there had a Liberation army.

During the next months, I collected more info, mainly by not switching the TV channel to another program whenever something about Kosovo came up. After six months of hesitation, I made my decision and I was ready to go.

The only way to join the Kosovo Liberation Army, or short KLA, was to go to Albania and find them there. I didn't know what politics they had regarding foreign volunteers, but I was willing to check it out. If there was no place for me, I would simply make my holiday on the Albanian seaside.

I took the train to Brindisi, Italy and from there a ferry to Albania. Albania was underdeveloped at best. I thought I was in Africa.

There was a lot of dust, it was incredibly hot and there were beggars everywhere. I finally found some KLA guys sitting in a bar near the city center of Tirana, their capital, and asked them how and if I could join their outfit. To my surprise, almost all of them spoke German or English.

They had migrated to Western Europe at a young age to find work and now they came back to liberate their homeland. Used to the living conditions of Berlin or Stockholm, they were even more appalled about the disorder in Albania than I was.

It turned out that there was already a handful of foreigners serving in the KLA's ranks and that their leadership seemed to be quite open-minded about this issue. I was invited to stay with them and join them. We stayed for another week in a small pension before we took a cab towards the border.

Infiltration

Our only problem was to slip through the mountainous border into Kosovo. We were getting our equipment in Northern Albania where they issued me a uniform, boots and, of course, a weapon. There were all kinds of rifles, but this time I decided not to go with an AK-47, but to try something new.

There was a brand new FAL rifle which looked good to me. The FAL is produced in Belgium, but this here was the Austrian copy of it. It had a stronger caliber than the AK and therefore more range; on the other hand, it required more care from its user and couldn't be handled as roughly as the Kalashnikov.

We had a lot of ammunition to carry, including warheads for anti-tank weapons and therefore we had to rely on horses to bring us over the mountain border. We got some small horses, ponies, and mules from the local farmers and off we went into the night.

The path through the so-called Albanian Alps was brutal. As our enemy controlled the main border passes and had a lot of patrols in the area, we could only use some very narrow paths that led us high into the mountains.

This happened to be very dangerous. We couldn't afford to make light and one wrong step could mean falling down a steep rock face. On our way up, one of our horses disappeared over the edge of the path. I thanked God that it was too dark for me to see how far it fell.

My ride was a little bit slow and I soon began to lose contact with the rest of my unit. Soon, I had to dismount and let my horse just carry my backpack and a wooden ammunition crate. After a couple of hours, the horse slowed down again and I had to carry my backpack myself.

Another hour later, I opened the ammunition crate and put all the rounds in my backpack. The horse and I had switched roles: I was carrying all the heavy shit now while my horse was leisurely walking behind me.

I started to sweat. When we were halfway through the mountains, our unit leader told us to take a break. We were now at a very high altitude, there were only rocks and stones and a strong wind was blowing. I started to feel cold, but it was unthinkable to light a fire. Although I was extremely tired from all the walking, I was glad when we continued our way.

The descent was much easier. The landscape began to become green again, the path widened and the danger from falling off a cliff was gone.

I mounted my horse again and this time it was almost enjoyable. We rode slowly and silently through forests and ravines, the sky was full of stars and all I could hear was the sound of my horse's hooves. I felt like I was in an adventure movie. Unforgettable!

Just before dawn, we reached a location where we met a local Guerrilla scout who would lead us deeper into the country. Our horses would stay there and return to Albania the next night with another guerrilla unit that was evacuating wounded fighters out of Kosovo.

We continued our way on foot, then later with a small lorry and after another three days, I reached the Guerrilla base where I would spend most of my time until the end of the war.

First Combat

Blerim was a tall and strong looking twenty-three year old soldier I had met during my stay in Albania. Despite his young age, he gave the impression of a serious and determined man. The hardships of the war had matured him. He had asked me in passable French if I would like to help him to set up a new unit in his village and I agreed immediately. I had another 'job offer' from some ex-con who ironically was in charge of the KLA's military police in one region, but I declined. I came here to fight and not to play policeman after all.

Blerim's village already had a few KLA units, but they were very badly organized and didn't look very reliable. Our new unit would recruit only young people from high school and college and we agreed upon that we didn't want any veterans from the former Yugoslav army in our ranks. This was a guerrilla war and I thought it would be easier to teach the principles of unconventional warfare to people with a 'blank sheet' than to someone who first had to unlearn all the things that he had once been taught in a regular army, before I could think of putting some new ideas in his head.

We found a handful of volunteers in the villages around and while Blerim took care of the logistics and administration stuff, I started with the training. We had no field manuals, but still, the instructions I taught to our soldiers were based on what I had once learned from field manuals, books and manual-based training, which I combined with my experience from Bosnia.

We made good progress and soon had a platoon-sized group of young, motivated, but still inexperienced fighters. Their fighting abilities would soon be put to the test.

One morning, we were alarmed that a small enemy force had entered the suburbs of a nearby city and had started to terrorize the local population. The Serbs went from door to door and demanded money or jewelry and the people who couldn't come up with any of it were brutally beaten up.

We took our jeeps and went there to check out the situation. Soon, we were engaged in a firefight with the enemy soldiers. It was urban warfare, house-to-house and our guys were doing a decent job.

I saw that our left side was very open and vulnerable and positioned myself there. Naim, one of our new soldiers, came with me. He still had a lot to learn, but he didn't talk much and was fearless. His codename was 'rabbit'.

My new buddy and I found ourselves in a very bad spot: While most of the fighting was going on a block away from us, our job was to secure a street to prevent an enemy attack from the flank. The enemy started shelling us with 82 mm mortars, but we had no cover to protect us. We couldn't enter any of the nearby buildings as they had no windows from where we could continue to observe the street. Additionally, there were high walls on both sides of the small alleyway where we were positioned.

The shells kept flying and we sat down with our backs against a wall, hoping for the best. Suddenly, I heard a very short and sharp "swoosh" sound. I put my head down to my knees, like you are advised to do in an aircraft emergency landing, and covered my head with my arms.

For half a second there was nothing. I couldn't hear, see or feel anything. Blank and empty space.

When I put my head up again, I saw that there was a lot of dust in the air. I checked my body and saw that there was blood coming out just above my right knee. Then I checked my buddy and although I couldn't see any blood, when I looked at his face, I saw that something was wrong:

I had seen this facial expression before when combat soldiers got wounded. It's as if their life has been sucked out of them: Pale face, mouth open, and the eyes unfocused and full of surprise.

He put his hand on his right shoulder and I saw that a blood stain started to appear on his jacket, slowly growing bigger. I helped him to take off his jacket to have a better look. This was serious, I could see a gaping hole near his clavicle. Inside the hole, one could see fragments of his collarbone.

We found some bandages and just plugged the hole with them. I told my buddy to stay still and ran off to find someone to help us. I didn't have to run more than fifty meters when a comrade showed up on the street. He told me there was an empty house where I could find cover from the artillery fire and that he would go to pick up my wounded comrade.

I found the house, entered it and took off my trousers. A piece of shrapnel had pierced the muscle above my right knee. There was blood, but it wasn't life-threatening. I decided to go back where I had left my wounded buddy and help with his evacuation. When I started to walk, I realized that I had problems to move. My right leg had become stiff and I could barely walk. When I was about to leave the house I saw that my two buddies were already nearby and so I didn't leave my shelter.

When we were all inside, we examined my comrade's wound again. Someone brought a first aid kit and another guy brought us some cake. It was a religious holiday and on their way to help us, some guys from our unit had been invited for coffee and cake by a local family.

After fifteen minutes, we left the house and hurried down the road where a jeep was waiting for us. Artillery and snipers were still firing at us. The driver explained that the situation had totally deteriorated: enemy troops, reinforced by tanks and armored vehicles, were trying to surround and attack us from the flank. Two of our soldiers had been killed.

All roads were blocked and the jeep went cross country. We were thoroughly shaken on the backseats and I hit my head several times when we went through a hole in the ground or hit a rock. I didn't care, though. I just wanted to get out!

The last meters before we left the suburb, I could see two armored vehicles rolling down the hill to our left. Fortunately, they were unable to shoot at us while they were on the move and we made a narrow escape.

My buddy was away from combat duty for about three months but eventually made a full recovery. I had only suffered a minor injury. After only a week, I was able to walk again. I attended the funeral of two KLA soldiers of another unit that had been killed on the same day.

Observations

We had a really shitty position and this was the reason why we got wounded. Surviving combat is all about being at the right place at the right time.

It's really not that difficult:

When you are shot at by direct fire (bullets, tanks, missiles) you better move your ass. On the other hand, when you are hit by indirect fire (artillery, grenade launchers), you stay where you are.

Still, many people don't get it: the shells are coming in closer and closer and they lose their nerve and get out of their position. The results are often fatal.

Or they get shot at and take cover in a really shitty position (like we did) where it will be just a matter of time until they will get hit. If they are not hit by direct fire immediately, then it will happen a few moments later by artillery. As soon as you are discovered and the enemy is taking aim at you, there is really no other choice than to get out. Always use cover fire when you make a move.

These are the most basic principles of small unit warfare. Unfortunately, the right behavior seems somehow to be counter-intuitive: hitting the ground is the most natural reaction when bullets are flying over your head. And who doesn't want to run away when the earth is exploding around them?

This is where the training kicks in. Soldiers have to overcome their natural instincts and have to do what has been proven right time after time on the battlefield. Only then will they have a chance to survive.

A Badass Escape

During the next weeks, the situation grew more tense and our unit got involved in numerous smaller skirmishes and firefights.

Although we were often busy fighting, we always continued the training. Give everyone a gun, quickly teach them how to use it and then send them into battle; those were my training objectives.

We didn't always have sufficient time to teach our recruits all the intricacies of infantry combat and sometimes, they would first go into battle and we would teach them the rest later.

Of course, these guys weren't the most efficient soldiers, but still, they could do some tasks. They would carry ammunition into the combat zone and wounded soldiers out of it. They were used as messengers or lookouts and we sent them away to get food, water, ammo or new radio batteries for us.

There are many combat related functions where such a guy might be useful. Even if you have already well trained new soldiers arriving in your unit, you will give them some easy tasks the first time they go into combat.

We would keep a close eye on these untrained newcomers and check out how they reacted under fire. When we saw that one of them was too scared to perform, we would send him back to where he came from without having wasted our time training him. In a way, sending them into battle first was a selection test.

Soon, our unit got a reputation. We were now officially assigned to function as the Quick Reaction Force on the brigade level. This meant that whenever there was a problem the other KLA units couldn't handle, they would call us for help.

Of course, after we were tasked with our new mission, we became even more active.

Early one morning, a group of enemy infantry had attacked our brigade's defense lines. We were alarmed over the radio and we immediately ran to the location on top of a hill.

When we approached the defense positions, we could see that the soldiers from our battalion had left them and were running down the hill in our direction. They probably thought: "Let the intervention group fight it out!"

One of my buddies stopped them. He spoke shortly with them and then the complete platoon that had just been ready to flee the frontline turned around and went back to fight. We were able to hold the line against a strong enemy and much to my surprise, the guys from the battalion did a decent job.

I was impressed with our soldier. He was the youngest soldier of our Kosovo Liberation Army unit, barely eighteen, and he had talked a whole platoon of much older soldiers into staying and fighting back. He had been into martial arts before the war and he was in very good shape. Everyone called him Tony, although that wasn't his real name. He was a quiet guy who spoke some English and we became friends instantly.

He later told me the following story:

Early on in the war, for whatever reasons, Tony decided that he needed a mobile phone. He changed into civilian clothes and went to the next city to buy one.

This was extremely dangerous and almost foolish: The Serbs, were ruling the cities and there was an arrest warrant out in his name. To make matters worse, he used to own a couple of shops in this city, prior to the war, and therefore everyone, including the Serb police and all local spies, would recognize his face.

Let him tell the story in his own words:

"I put some civilian clothes on and walked the ten miles from the base into the city. Everything went smoothly and nobody seemed to recognize me until I entered a small three-story shopping mall in the city center. Just when I had passed the main entrance, I saw two plainclothes cops-and they saw me, too! They were sticking their heads together while looking at me and probably, they were telling each other:

"You see that guy? Is that really him? Can he be that stupid to walk around here?

While they evaluated my stupidity level, I went to the stairway and arrived at the first floor. I could look downstairs and still see the two cops: one of them was talking over the radio now, probably calling for reinforcements.

I didn't know what to do and so I decided I could as well continue my shopping. I went to the third floor and entered a small mobile phone shop. The shop owner was a good friend of mine and I told him about my trouble with the cops coming after me.

He told me that there was a back entrance to the mall and if I hurried, I could make it out of there before the police could get me.

I left the shop immediately. I looked downstairs to the main entrance, but I couldn't see the two cops anymore. While I descended the stairs, I could hear police sirens coming from the backside of the building: these fuckers were trying to cut me off!

I decided to risk everything and walk out of the main entrance. They wouldn't expect me to do that and I might have a small chance to surprise them.

I slowly walked out and as I almost started to think that I had made it, someone grabbed my arm from behind. I turned around and, of course, it was one of the civilian cops.

He said: "Are you Tony?" and I answered: "What you think, you idiot?" Of course, he knew me. I used to own a fisherman's supply shop and this guy used to be one of my best customers. Now he was asking me stupid questions.

I was extremely worried: it was war and I was one of the most wanted 'terrorists'. Getting arrested by the cops was equal to getting killed, but only after being tortured for a couple of days by the infamous Serbian Secret Intelligence Service.

Somehow I managed to stay calm, though. My voice didn't betray me while my little conversation with the enemy went on:

The cop: "You have to come with us to the police station!"

Me: "No, you guys have to come to my station!"

Cop: "What station?"

Me: "We are going to (the name of our guerrilla base)!"

These guys were playing for time. They thought that I was armed and didn't want to get into trouble with me until reinforcements had arrived. Unfortunately, I had left my pistol at the base and the only weapon I had with me was a hand grenade. No way, I could use it in this situation! I could hear now police sirens coming from everywhere. I was running out of time and had to do something!

As I looked down the street, I saw a familiar looking car: two local mafia guys were parking their Mercedes a couple of yards away from me. I knew these guys from high school and I was sure they had a gun with them in the car which I could use to shoot my way out.

I started to walk over to them, but the cop still had my arm. I pushed his hand away and told him that I would just go to the car of my friends and tell them to call my family to tell them I was at the police station. The cops didn't know what to do and before they could stop me, I was sitting in the car, door closed and telling the two Mafiosi to give me their gun.

These two blokes didn't realize the trouble I was in and were starting to make small talk with me: "Hey man, long time no see! Wanna take a ride with us? We take you anywhere you want!"

I almost screamed at them: "I need a fucking gun, right now!"

They said that they were unarmed and I left the car from the other side, away from the cops. I started running while at the same I was fishing for the hand grenade in one of my jacket pockets.

Just when I had put my hand on the grenade, the first cop grabbed my arm again. I swung around and punched my fist with the grenade in it right into his face. He went down immediately.

By now, the second cop had pulled his gun out and was getting ready to shoot me. I ran as fast as I could! While I was running, I saw the shop windows to my right side shattering. The cop was shooting and running after me at the same time. Lucky for me, he wasn't very accurate.

I turned left into a small alleyway and the cop was close behind me. I ran and ran, but after two hundred yards the road ended and there was a high brick wall. I was trapped!

The cop realized that I had nowhere to go and stopped running. He aimed the pistol at me and just when I thought that he was going to pull the trigger, I saw his colleague approaching us. He had recovered from my punch and looked really pissed off! No doubt, it would be his privilege and honor to kill me and therefore the other cop took his gun down for a moment to wait for his buddy to catch up with him and then kill me.

I thought: "Now or never!" and raised both of my hands. While my right hand held the grenade, my left hand's index finger was around the ring of the grenade.

Both cops froze, I had their full attention. I pulled the grenade's ring and started talking: "If I go down, I'll take you motherfuckers with me!"

We had a stand-off: If they shot me, I would release the lever of the grenade and we would probably all die. And if I threw the grenade, they would have ample time to shoot me before the grenade would explode.

I took a look at the grenade in my hand and was shocked: the ring hadn't pulled the pin out of the grenade as it normally should, but it just had broken off from the pin. This grenade, when thrown, wouldn't explode at all! Thank god, the two cops didn't seem to realize that my grenade had a major malfunction, but sooner or later they would.

Time to act! I stepped forward and made a move as if I was going to throw the grenade at them. To my surprise, instead of shooting their guns, both cops threw themselves to the ground immediately.

I turned around and checked the wall behind me: very difficult to climb, but possible. I stepped a few yards back, ran towards the wall, jumped and got a grip on the top of the wall! I lifted myself over it and started running again.

Cops were everywhere now, but it started to get dark and I made it to the outskirts of the town where I arrived at the bank of a river. I jumped inside and swam to the other side.

I was safe! I couldn't believe my luck! I slowly started walking to our base and thought about what had just happened. Unlike when I talked to the cops, my nerves were showing now. I started shaking and had to sit down for a while to calm down. After a while, I could continue walking and I made it back to our base early in the morning."

Christmas Carols

The end of the year was approaching and so I organized a Christmas party. I always loved celebrating Christmas, but in Kosovo, without electricity and no money to spend on preparations, celebrating Christmas proved to be a challenge.

Our unit's base was in a small mountain village and although there was a war going on, children still went to school. There was only one teacher who gave lessons for every age and on every subject.

About one month before the big holiday, the school teacher had invited me to his modest home for a cup of tea. We were making small talk and he had a lot of questions about life in Germany. Somehow, we started talking about Christmas traditions and although he was a Muslim like most of the villagers, he became very interested. I told him all I knew and he seemed to like it.

On my way back to the base, I was thinking about the upcoming holidays. I shared my thoughts with one of my buddies who had previously lived in France and we decided to organize a small celebration for Christmas.

First of all, we needed a Christmas tree! The only pine trees were planted behind the schoolyard and so we took an axe, went there, picked the most beautiful one and my buddy started cutting it.

The teacher, alarmed by the noise, came out of the small school building, saw what we did and got very angry. Those were the school's pine trees and they were not to be touched! My buddy stopped chopping, but I told him to continue.

In my opinion, the school and all its pine trees would be burned down to rubble the day our enemy entered the village. Better to take a tree now and have some nice time with it.

An argument over the tree ensued. One moment, my buddy was chopping and the next moment, he stopped. Finally, we compromised. The school teacher promised to help us preparing our festivities, but only if we would let the pine tree in its place.

We went back to our base. During the next days, the teacher invited me again and asked me detailed questions about the things we would need for our little event.

Two days before Christmas, I took some soldiers from our unit and went to some abandoned houses to look for something that we could use as a tree decoration. I found some aluminum foil, little toys, walnuts and much other stuff.

My buddy found some candles! We had no electricity and without enough candles, we would be doomed.

One night before Christmas, we went back to the school, but this time with a saw. While I was the lookout, my buddy went to work on the tree. The teacher had given us the permission to stage our event in his school and so we had to carry our pine tree just around the building and put it inside.

Finally, the great day had arrived! We went two hours earlier to start decorating the room and the tree, and when we arrived there, we were in for a surprise:

The teacher had kept his word and more than that. A small lorry was parked inside the schoolyard and people were unloading food and drinks from it. I always thought that our celebration would be more or less symbolic, due to the lack of almost everything, but now it looked like we would have a really good party.

An hour later, the first guests arrived. Those were all battle-hardened guerrilla fighters, but when they entered the nicely decorated room and saw the really beautiful tree, we could see it on their faces that they were more than a little surprised and amazed.

We started eating and drinking, my buddy cracked some jokes and then we attempted to sing a Christmas carol. This ended in failure and a big laughter.

Our teacher was sitting in the 'seat of honor' at the end of the table and looked really happy. He was smiling at everybody. I think he knew that we had cut 'his' tree, but he didn't say anything. Maybe he had already forgiven us our little crime.

After all, it was Christmas.

Miguel

For the New Year, we had a special guest. One morning, there was a group of reporters waiting outside our base. Five journalists from different international media pushing each other to get an exclusive interview with Blerim, our commander.

My buddy Tony told me later: "Our commander told me to go outside and pick one journalist for the interview. When I went to the gate and saw all these journalists blocking the entry and talking like crazy, I noticed a skinny guy at the other side of the street, calmly smoking a cigarette. This guy didn't even look up when I announced that only one of them would be allowed to enter the base. I pointed my finger at him and told him to come inside: He was the only one not breaking my balls."

Miguel was his name. He was a Spanish cameraman working for the Associated Press. Before he had come to Kosovo he had covered the war in Bosnia. I later learned that he has also been a member of a Spanish Special Forces unit.

We all had a very good relationship with Miguel, right from day one. As he had been a soldier himself, he knew how to move around and never stood in the way while filming our operations. Many reporters would be arrogant and bothered us with stupid questions ("What did he say? What did he say now?"). Miguel didn't talk much, but when he did, it was short and to the point.

After a while, we became accustomed to his presence and he practically became a member of our unit. When the roads were bad or it was too late for him to return to his office, he would sleep at our base.

I would often talk to him, not only about the war in Kosovo, but about military and political topics, good food and drinks, and even about literature (he admired Graham Greene) and philosophy. One day we had a long conversation about the best whiskey brands. Whatever he did, he was always thoughtful, calm and friendly.

On Guerrilla Warfare

Time passed quickly. After more than a half year of being a guerrilla, I began to understand what guerrilla warfare was about.

We only moved in small groups. We often had nobody giving us orders and it was all up to our own initiative if, when and where we attacked the enemy.

In such a guerrilla war, the big cities and the roads connecting them belong to the enemy. The guerrilla holds the mountains and the forests. That means that we had to walk a lot in very rough terrain.

You'll operate in small groups mostly at night. There are no frontal battles although sometimes a bigger guerrilla force will be assembled to keep the enemy from advancing into strategically important territory.

Under the cover of darkness, we planted a lot of anti-tank mines and improvised explosives to stop the advance of the enemy. Usually, we went out in a small group and tried to attack a lesser defended enemy position or ambush a military patrol.

All the conveniences that a modern Western army offers to its soldiers, even during a war, didn't exist. There was no hospital. If we had a wounded soldier we had to carry him at night to an improvised hospital, about 25 kilometers away. The time would soon come when we had to make this trip every night.

These improvised hospitals often had to be evacuated due to approaching enemy forces. Then the whole medical staff had to carry somehow all their patients to the mountains and stay there in improvised shelters to wait out the enemy attack.

Therefore, soldiers who were lightly wounded often decided to stay with their units. This was safer: You knew the guys and often you even had your family nearby.

Food was scarce. Although I was lucky enough not to suffer from starvation (other units did however), sometimes our food supplies were really down to almost nothing. Additionally, there were a lot of civilian refugees in the mountains and the KLA had to supply them with food.

The Serbs didn't allow humanitarian organizations to bring food to these refugees so it was up to us. One night we assembled all the vehicles we could find and went to a big food warehouse in enemy territory. There the Serbs had stocked the food from the humanitarian aid organizations. The enemy didn't expect us to go there and there were no guards to stop us. We got about 25 tons of supply, enough to get through for a couple of weeks. We did a lot of similar, but smaller actions to get more food and other supplies, like gas for the few jeeps we had.

Every two or three days we sent out some soldiers to scout for a cow. Whole villages were deserted and before the villagers fled they set all their animals free. The Serbian army usually killed all livestock they could find, not to eat it, but to deprive the KLA or anybody else from taking it. This was part of their ethnic cleansing campaign.

But when you are moving around all the time, there is only so much food that you can carry. Sometimes we could catch a chicken and cook it, but usually, we were eating noodles. After some long days of fighting and marching, we were often too tired to light a fire and cook something. In those cases, it was just bread and water.

Of course, we almost never had any electrical power. For a time we had generators, but you can't take them with you: Every time we had to move we tried to hide them as good as possible.

You become an expert in hiding and camouflaging stuff. Everything you can't take with you has to be hidden. Even weapons were carefully packed in plastic bags and hidden underground.

There was no such thing as a holiday, no rest and recreation. When there is a calm moment you are busy with cleaning your equipment, washing your clothes or catching some sleep.

Most of the time, there was no chance to sleep. Being on the move all the time, never knowing what is going to happen the next moment tended to mess with your sleeping pattern.

Even if you could find a quiet place to sleep somewhere you would hear faint 'popping' noises far away in the distance, when enemy artillery started shooting and then you were waiting for the incoming artillery shells. You started counting the seconds till impact, trying to calculate the distance between you and the artillery. Then you tried to figure out where the shells were hitting: "200 meters away? 150? Are they getting closer?" This could go on day and night.

You learn to improvise. We were lucky to have some very capable guys in our unit who could fix almost anything with tape and wire. One of them helped me attach a self-made grenade launcher to my assault rifle.

Our enemy was totally superior to us in numbers and in material. We had the better morale and we knew the terrain, but there is only so much that you can achieve with that. Once we were called upon to defend against an enemy attack of 35 enemy tanks- and we didn't even have 35 soldiers. So it was always David against Goliath, but one gets used to it.

The only problem when you are up against these numbers is, that there is a very high risk of being cut off and getting surrounded. So all the time you have to plan how to escape. But even with all the planning, it happened that we found ourselves with no way out. Then you wait for the night, pray for the best and slip through the enemy's line.

Despite all the dangers and hardship, being a guerrilla was also rewarding. We were with the people and part of a big liberation force.

The Ambush

One day, one of our soldiers came to me and told me that his home village was occupied by the Serbian army and that all civilians had fled. This village was in the North of Kosovo, deep into enemy territory and far away from any of our positions. We decided to check it out.

We assembled a small team of five soldiers, including a machine gunner, a sniper and a guy with a 40mm multiple grenade launcher (MGL). We also took two M 72 RPGs with us and some military explosives. We kept our preparations silent. Only our unit commander was informed about what we were up to.

On a late winter afternoon, we started to march towards the village. As the enemy held all roads and had checkpoints and observation posts at all strategic points, we had to move through very rough terrain, mostly wood and underbrush.

We had to advance very slowly and therefore soon got tired. As soon as night fell down, we dared to take a small secondary road to bring us closer to our target. This was very dangerous as there was military traffic on this road. Every time we saw the headlights of an approaching car, we jumped for cover. Still, we covered some ground and reached our destination in the early morning hours. It was still dark and we carefully went from house to house. The whole village had been burned down, there wasn't a single building that was spared by the enemy. We finally found an annex building of a small farm that was intact and tried to catch some sleep. Of course, this was nearly impossible as we were all too wired up. Every time I heard a noise my pulse went up.

With the first daylight, we got a better view of the situation: The village had been abandoned. It was right next to the main road which happened to be an important enemy supply route from Serbia to Kosovo. We decided to set up an ambush, but first of all, we needed to eat. There were still enough chickens running around the place so we caught one, made a small fire and roasted it. This was dangerous; we could make out an enemy position about one kilometer away from the village. We were careful not to make any noise or smoke.

Stomachs full, we found a good position near the road and waited. Moments before we had found this position we had observed some Serbian paramilitaries that had gone down the road with a small truck. Two guys were in the driver's cabin and three more on the open back. As we were not ready yet for an attack when they had passed us coming down the road, we now hoped that we would catch them on their way back. We waited for about two hours. There was only civilian traffic on the road. Finally, we heard the small truck coming back. This time its back was loaded with all kinds of stuff: TV sets and furniture, stolen from abandoned ethnic Albanian villages. A paramilitary was sitting on top of all the stolen goods, smoking a cigarette and expecting no evil.

When the truck was passing in front of us, we opened fire. The guy on the back of the truck was hit immediately by our machine gun. The driver steered the truck off the road and it overturned. Two paramilitaries ran into a nearby cornfield and got away.

Meanwhile, a civilian car turned up and stopped fifty meters away from the truck. The driver also ran away in the cornfield. Two more civilian cars turned up and backed away.

We kept the road blocked for an hour. Then we heard an armored convoy approaching us. The enemy thought we were long gone and therefore started to shoot with tanks at the nearby hills where they suspected our escape route to be.

We withdrew towards the enemy positions we had spotted earlier on. It was a line of trenches, but surprisingly they were unmanned. We booby-trapped them.

Then we went into a nearby forest and waited until late afternoon. The enemy continued strafing the hills with tanks and artillery, but we were safe and didn't engage.

Then we decided to try our luck down the road from where the enemy column had been approaching us before. We chose a path parallel to the road. We continued about two kilometers, but the enemy convoy was long gone.

We decided to set up another ambush: There was an excellent position at a small building near the road where we could put our machine gunner in a relatively protected place. One of our guys went further down the road to tell us via radio if any enemy forces were approaching.

For a while, nothing happened and we got bored. But finally, our observer told us about a big bus coming up the road. We didn't know if it was civilian or military, so we decided not to attack it. I went to the road to have a good look. Our position was a little bit elevated so I had a straight look at its passengers as the bus slowly passed by: All of them were Serbian soldiers. I could see their shaved heads when they passed by two meters away from me, many of them dozing away or smoking.

It was already too late to attack them, so we let them pass. This was very frustrating: It would have been an enormous success to get this bus. Now it was beginning to get really dark. Our chances to mount another ambush were getting very slim as the enemy rarely moved at night. Tired and frustrated I walked up and down the tarmac with one of my comrades. It was almost night now and we were almost ready to leave the place when our radio crackled: Our observer reported two jeeps approaching. Definitely military.

We positioned ourselves again: I stood behind a bush when the first jeep passed: A black Land Rover with a mounted machine gun on its roof. The machine gunner pointed his weapon straight at me when he passed, but couldn't see me in the half dark. They were Special Forces!

Seconds later, our machine gunner opened fire. The first jeep was rippled by bullets. The jeep's machine gun opened fire, but only for a second, then the gunner got hit. Now the second jeep passed us. Land Rover again, but no machine gun. While I shot with my AK-47, my comrade shot an MGL grenade. It hit the back of the Land Rover, but didn't explode: The MGL 40mm grenade has a security mechanism: A target has to be more than 15 meters away for the grenade to explode. We were too close. So we ran a few meters down the tarmac away from the jeeps and my buddy shot again. This time the grenade went off and the second jeep got severely damaged.

Our observer told us that more enemy was approaching us. Time to leave! I ordered the machine gunner to cease fire so that we could safely withdraw, but the guy didn't hear me. I shouted for a minute and finally, he stopped shooting.

Tired and low on ammo we decided to go back to our base. We climbed the nearby hills and found some local villagers there who had fled from the Serbian army a few days earlier. After we smoked a cigarette with them one of them helped us to find a way back to friendly territory. This is most important when operating in enemy territory. If you have somebody with you who knows the ground it makes things much easier. Early the next morning we reached our base. I was happy but very tired. I hadn't slept for two nights and we had walked maybe 70 kilometers through rough terrain.

Observations:

Ambushes were an important part of our tactics. Through them, we were provided with weapons and badly needed ammunition.

Setting up an ambush is a difficult task, so let's keep it simple: Let's say, you want to attack a truck which is carrying food and other supplies to an enemy outpost on a nearby hill.

Timing. You want to ambush the truck on his way to the outpost. It will be loaded and going uphill and is therefore a slower and easier target to hit.

Forces. To succeed you need overwhelming firepower. Overkill is preferred. Don't attack an enemy company when you only have a squad.

Split your team. You need at least one group that executes the attack and another that will provide cover fire.

Scouts. Send a guy down the road to tell you when your truck is coming. This soldier can also tell you if the truck is escorted by other vehicles. If you can spare more men, send one up the hill in the direction of the outpost.

Location. Very important! Choose a place for your ambush where the target has to slow down (sharp bends, uphill). The place also must provide you with enough cover so you can't be seen by your target or other vehicles which might pass by. And of course, you need to be covered from enemy fire as well: your cover fire team especially needs to have a good spot. You also must be able to withdraw safely from your ambush after the attack.

Reassembly point. You need a place where everyone assembles after the ambush. This place should be at least one kilometer away from your ambush site and on your planned escape route.

Attack. Make clear on whose command you'll open fire. If you have mines or IED's you can use them to stop the truck.

Everybody in your team has to know their job: The cover team needs to know which zones to cover and the attacking team should be informed on who goes where; for example, one guy to the driver's side, one guy to the opposite side and two to the back of the truck.

Speed is *everything*. You have to surprise your enemy. Go in, shoot everyone who doesn't surrender immediately, take weapons, ammo and whatever else you may need and get the hell out of there. Weapons and ammo that you can't take with you have to be destroyed. You can set the truck on fire if you have the time.

Retreat. Everyone must get to the reassembly point as fast as possible. The attack team always withdraws first while being covered. If the ambush has been a success and you are not under fire, don't bother with counting your men; you are wasting your time.

Regroup at the reassembly point. Assess the situation and decide who is carrying all the stuff you got from the truck.

This is a basic outline of an ambush, but it covers all the main elements. In reality, most of our ambushes were not planned at all. After a while, you become more experienced and you are able to react quickly to a promising situation: You see an enemy convoy approaching and you decide to set up an ambush. In a few seconds the ambush is set up, half a minute later you open fire and another minute later you have already disappeared.

Anyway, ambushes rarely go as planned and you start improvising immediately after the first shot is fired.

Some important tips:

It is extremely easy to get shot by your own soldiers while executing an ambush. Often you attack at night and things can get messy. Therefore, every soldier in the team must be extremely careful.

As soon as you start your attack, there is no way back. You have to be decisive, fast and deadly. There is absolutely no time for hesitation. Sometimes, when we ambushed Serbian infantry units, these guys managed to shoot back at us. If you allow the enemy to get the upper hand, they will eliminate your attack team.

Never underestimate your opponent! Some troops are very good at defending against an ambush. I found that British soldiers especially react very quickly and professionally in these type of situations. And many infantries work with ambush spotters. These are soldiers that walk in front of the main troops on both roadsides to detect ambushes. Always be careful!

24 Days of Combat

After the New Year, everybody started talking about a new massive Serbian offensive. Their plan, so we were informed, was to crush all resistance, to round up the civilian population and then to kick everyone out of the country. To do that, massive amounts of troops had to be brought into their positions.

Soon, we were to have our first contact with them.

One day in early February, our platoon was alarmed by the news that a large enemy force was approaching our base. The enemy was about five or six kilometers away and had stopped at a small village.

We had basically no forces out there, so our platoon had to hurry up to stop them. The ground was very rough and there was snow, therefore we couldn't use our jeeps, but had to run there instead.

We arrived on top of a hill about 500 meters away from the village, split up into three groups and positioned ourselves in some empty farmhouses. Somehow the enemy had spotted our arrival and immediately started shooting with machine guns from the nearby village.

Five minutes later, mortar shells started coming in. I was standing in an empty room with a window looking towards the enemy village when a bullet tore the window frame apart. I almost got hit in the face by a big wooden splinter. I was looking for cover in the corridor when I saw this guy hunkering down in a corner. He looked at me and said, trembling: "Oh man, I'm so scared!"

To be honest, that day we all were, but we continued fighting.

The enemy's continuing small arms fire forced my fellow comrades who had been in the other rooms to come and join us in the corridor. We were now five guys, hunching down and waiting for the bullets and shells to stop.

To make sure that no enemy was sneaking up on us, every couple minutes I would go into the room, take a glimpse out of the window and return back to the corridor.

For a while, not much happened. The mortar fire continued and more and more gunfire erupted. We stayed put in the corridor and we were smoking cigarettes: There was nothing else to do.

After a while, I entered the room just another time, took another look outside the window and was baffled. There was a tank just outside of the window! It had approached from the left side of the building where I had a blind angle, stopped in front of my window and now slowly turned its cannon towards me. It was so close, I could see every scratch on its black hull.

I was completely surprised: I didn't even know that our enemy had deployed any tanks that day. Covered by the noise of the shooting and artillery fire, the tank had approached us without being heard.

We had no anti-tank weapons with us, so there was only one solution: Get out as fast as you can! There was a small window in the corridor which allowed us to get away from the enemy and we quickly jumped out. Outside, I took a look around and spotted another squad from my unit which was also leaving their position in another building.

I needed their RPG, but they told me that two of their soldiers had taken it and were trying to attack the tank from the flank.

I saw that one soldier had a video camera, so I took it and went around the house to film the tank. I couldn't shoot it with a weapon, but at least I could get some nice video footage. There was a hedge and some haystacks where I could hide and I started making a little frontline video.

After that, I went to look for the guys who had the RPG. I found them and we went after the tank. One guy aimed and shot and although he hit the target, the tank continued to move.

After a while, however, it stopped and slowly retreated. Its crew had obviously decided to wait for their infantry to join up.

We were done there. We didn't have nearly enough soldiers and we withdrew about 300 meters to a more favorable position. After a while, another KLA unit came to our help. The Serbs once again advanced with a single tank and started hitting our new positions. A tank shell hit our position ten meters to my left and injured one of my comrades. But that was it. We were able to hold our ground and the enemy's attacks came to a standstill.

When we returned to our base I took a look at my videotape. While I got some nice footage from the hedge, I somehow forgot to push the "RE-CORD" button the moment my comrade was shooting at the tank. The poor guy was really disappointed. He thought he could show his friends some really cool combat footage, but the crucial five seconds were missing from the tape.

Still, we were glad that we had survived a very serious situation and that nobody was seriously injured. I also met the guy who had told me that he's been scared while we were in the corridor of that house. He told me what had happened to him after we had left him:

"I was scared that an artillery shell would hit the house, but at the same time I didn't dare leave my hiding place as there were thousands of bullets hitting the walls of the building. I was alone; everybody else was outside fighting. I felt ashamed that I wasn't there with my comrades, but I couldn't get myself to move.

After what seemed an eternity, the fighting outside slowed down. Now another terrifying thought crossed my mind: "What if the enemy advances and finds me here?" I was still not sure on what to do, but after another minute I ran out of the building. I couldn't see anybody outside and I began to freak out.

I kept running and running. Only after I was totally exhausted, I allowed myself to stop. I didn't know for how long I'd kept running, but when I looked around me I realized that I wasn't only out of the fighting zone, but I had completely left the area where our brigade was operating!

I immediately turned around. I was very ashamed of myself and also scared that somebody would see me and ask me what the hell I was doing there, miles away from my unit. It started to get dark and I continued my way back to our base, avoiding all villages and inhabited places."

Frankly, I was surprised by the guy's honesty. We later decided that he would stay in our unit. As he obviously wasn't a fighter, we put him in our support squad which was tasked with non-combat duties, like cooking or maintenance.

The next time we went into battle, I made sure that I had an RPG with me. In the end, I came here to fight and not to make movies. In the following months, we encountered many more tanks and I had plenty of opportunities to shoot at tanks.

Night Attack

Our enemy was warned that they had to expect heavy resistance if they would continue their approach towards our base, but we could only delay, not stop them. They had positioned a couple of tanks in an isolated forward base on a hill close to our valley. From their new position, they were able to observe our movements and shoot directly at our base. We had to do something!

In a late afternoon, I went with Blerim on a reconnaissance mission. We had a small video camera with us and were able to film the enemy's outpost from several different angles.

Back at our Kosovo Liberation Army base, we watched and re-watched our videotape and made a plan. We would attack in two groups: The first one with several machine guns would approach the enemy from the left flank and shoot suppressing fire.

Their mission was to make it impossible for the enemy's tank crews to get out of their positions and enter their tanks. This was crucial: If the enemy would be able to operate their tanks, both of our attack groups would be extremely vulnerable.

The second assault team which I was a part of, was much smaller. We were only three fighters and our job was to get into a good position in order to shoot at the tanks. To achieve our task, we carried two 'Zolja' RPGs (Rocket Propelled Grenades) and a bigger 90 mm 'OSA' RPG.

We left our base at midnight and marched on foot towards the enemy's position. On our way were several villages which we didn't dare to enter. We didn't know if they were occupied by enemy troops or not, and we also had to be careful not to encounter any enemy patrols.

Five hundred meters in front of our target, we split into two teams. The first attack group went to the left, while my own small detachment slowly climbed up the hill, straight to the location where we had seen the enemy tanks in the afternoon. There were a lot of small trees which gave us some concealment. It wouldn't protect us from enemy fire, though.

The last meters we walked very slowly. There was a hedge in front of us where we kneeled down to plan our next moves. We talked in whispers: My buddies would take a center and right position, while I would go a little to the left. We saw two tanks and decided that the one that was further away from us would be attacked with the stronger 'OSA' rocket, while the other tank would fall victim to our 'Zoljas'.

I had the 'Zolja' and prepared it to shoot. The 'OSA' would shoot first and that would be the signal, not only for the RPGs but also for the first assault team, to open fire.

I stood up and waited. My target was about fifty meters away from me and I hoped that no Serb would decide to go for a smoke at this time. We knew there were guards somewhere, but they were further to my left. Our first assault team would have to deal with them.

I stood still and listened. A flash of light and a loud 'boom' to my right. The 'OSA'! My ears rang when I aimed and activated the firing button on my RPG. I was shortly blinded by the trail of my rocket, but then I could see it exploding about thirty meters in front of me. It had hit an obstacle before it had reached its target!

I was disappointed, but there was no time for regrets. Hell broke loose! Our first team was shooting at the enemy's outpost and I could hear a few bullets zipping over my head. I put away the empty tube of my RPG and made my AK-47 ready. Then I waited if I could see the muzzle flashes of an enemy weapon. After a few seconds, I saw a little flash to my left and started shooting.

I shot three burst, knelt down and looked what my two buddies were doing. The 'OSA' gunner looked at me and gave me a sign to follow him. He had made his shot and there was no reason for us to stay around any longer. Any second, our enemy might recover from the shock and return fire. We had to get away as quickly as possible!

Our second 'Zolja' gunner had already left us and we met him a few minutes later near an empty farmhouse at the bottom of the hill. I told him that I missed my shot and he said that he might have hit the tank, but wasn't sure.

Apparently, our 'OSA' had hit its target and had taken the tank down. We were happy! A few moments later, our first assault team joined us. They had met only very little resistance and had no problems to deal with it.

Most importantly, no one was dead or injured.

We left the place heading to our base, but after only a couple of meters, we came under heavy machine gun fire from the top of the hill. 12.7 mm tracer rounds were hitting the ground a few meters away from us. Most probably, this was the anti-aircraft machine gun from one of the tanks.

We started running, but the bullets didn't stop. I was wondering if they could see us or if they were just extremely lucky. We ran up another smaller hill and when we crossed the ridge we were finally safe!

We made a quick headcount and fortunately, everyone was there with us. Miraculously, nobody was injured. We continued our way, this time much more relaxed, and reached our base without further incidents.

Observations

After you have spent a couple of weeks outdoors, without any artificial light sources, you will find out that your eyes have adjusted and that your ability to see at night has improved considerably.

You will be able to move around swiftly and do all the tasks with the same ease as in daylight. Of course, at night you see less, but you will learn to operate your weapons and equipment not by seeing, but by feeling things. You will memorize where you put all your stuff, and be able to find everything easily when you need it.

Guerrilla armies prefer to operate at night, and many of them have no night vision equipment. Sometimes, when we were under a daytime attack, I looked at my watch and desperately wished for the dark to come to get a break from the fighting, regroup and eventually to strike back.

Crossing the mountains at the border to Albania had only been possible to do at night. From the very first day of the war, every fighter knew that the night belonged to us.

At night we could send people out into enemy controlled territory to look for food and other supplies. We were able to transport our wounded soldiers to field hospitals which were often far away from our areas of operation. Most importantly, we used the cover the night offered in order to approach enemy positions for surprise attacks, and to also mine and booby-trap their supply routes.

The night is the guerrilla's best friend.

Explosives

As the main attack on our base was now only days away, we laid anti-personnel and anti-tank mines on every possible approach route. Some of these mines were activated by electric wire so that we had to leave a soldier nearby to detonate them. We dug out trenches and bunkers to provide cover and protection for these soldiers.

Most of our mining activity was done by night. It turned out that handling explosives in the dark can be as dangerous as a firefight at daytime.

We decided to set out into the night to lay a booby trap in front of a Serbian checkpoint. It was a moonless night with lots of cloud cover and black dark. There was an abandoned Albanian village near this checkpoint and I went there with Tony, one of our most fearless fighters, to prepare for our mission. We went to the basement of a half-destroyed house and started to unpack the explosives from my backpack.

Tony lit a candle and I put a hand grenade fuse into a massive block of TNT. We had removed most part of its safety lever beforehand, so that the fuse would nicely fit in a hole that we drilled into the explosive.

I pulled the safety pin halfway out. This way, after we connected the pull ring with a tripwire, the device would be activated by a slight touch on the wire.

Then we put a lot of tape around the device to make sure that the fuse would stay in place when the pin was pulled out. We had done similar tasks a couple of times before, both day and night, but never in absolute darkness.

We were about a mile away from the enemy and slowly walked towards their position. There was a small side road that led to the checkpoint where we had spotted enemy patrols during the day.

Our idea was that a patrol left the checkpoint, ran into the wire and activated the device. Due to the delay of the hand grenade fuse, the explosive charge would explode three seconds later, just in time when half of the patrol had passed by.

We came to the end of the road near the checkpoint and decided that this was a good spot. Tony pulled out some wire from his pockets and attached one end to a tree on the roadside. I would tape the explosive device to another tree on the opposite side of the road and we would connect it to the wire.

When I attached the explosive to the tree I encountered the first problem: The duct tape made a loud "phhhht" sound, when I pulled it from the tape roll and there were also small electrical sparks from static energy.

The enemy was too close and would hear and see us. Therefore I had to go back around a corner, take some tape from the roll and then go back to tape the device to the tree.

Explosives finally attached to the tree, my friend gave me the end of the wire and I began to connect it to the pull ring. This was a delicate job: I wanted to have maximum tension on the wire so that the pin would be pulled out by the slightest touch of the wire. I also didn't want the wire to hang too loose (and low) in order to avoid a dog, or some other animal, activating the device. On the other hand, too much tension and the pin would come out by itself or by a blow of wind.

I almost finished my job when I felt that the wire had too much tension and had started pulling the pin out! I immediately put both of my hands around the fuse to hold down the rest of the security lever and to prevent the whole thing from blowing up. I told Tony to cut the wire. He immediately grasped the seriousness of the situation, pulled the wire in my direction and the tension on the wire slacked.

While I continued to have both of my hands around the fuse, he pulled out his pocket knife and first cut the wire and then removed the explosive from the tree. We asked ourselves what to do. There was no way that we could just throw the whole device away and get out of it unharmed.

The only solution was to go back to the village and defuse our device. While I still had my hands around the fuse, my friend put his hands under the explosives to carry them. We had to coordinate our movements carefully and we didn't dare to stumble or fall.

After what seemed like an eternity we arrived at the house and went straight to the basement. We put the explosives on the ground and Tony lit up a candle. Now we could take a closer look at our device. The pin was almost completely out of the fuse and the security lever had already begun to move a little upwards. I pushed the lever a tiny bit down and my friend tried to put the pin back in, but without success. Due to my constant pressure on the fuse, the pin was deformed and didn't fit in anymore.

We decided not to risk anymore and to separate the fuse from the explosives. Tony took out his knife again and carefully cut around my hands through the duct tape. We tried again and this time the pin went back into the fuse.

Now we needed a break! We smoked a cigarette with shaking hands and marveled at our luck. Then we took another detonator and repeated the whole procedure. The mission wasn't over yet. This time, however, we wouldn't risk that much anymore and installed the device at a considerable distance to the enemy. We went back to our base, told our comrades the story and then went to sleep. The next time we were sure to be more careful.

It wasn't the enemy that made our night scary, but our own negligence.

Delay Tactics

The Serbs started their operation with a massive artillery barrage. Two days prior to the attack, they had flown a spy plane over our village to photograph our defense positions. Their artillery fire was therefore directed at our trenches. Some of our bunkers got direct hits. Thankfully nobody was inside them, as they were used only to launch attacks on an approaching enemy. No KLA soldier got wounded; we were either in safe positions inside the village or in the small bunkers near the enemy's approach routes.

Our attack and retreat tactic slowed down the enemy, but after two days, the first enemy tanks approached our village. Meanwhile, as the neighboring villages had come into the enemy's hands, we came under attack from three different directions.

We decided to mine and to booby trap the complete village. All civilians were evacuated and our zone headquarters had moved to another place deep in the mountains. We had nothing to lose anymore.

During the night, under the cover of darkness, we placed anti-tank mines very close to the enemy's tank positions. Surprisingly, the Serbs decided that the first vehicle to enter our village would be a truck with infantry. It immediately rolled over an anti-tank mine at the entry of our village and blew up. A second infantry truck approached to help the survivors of the first attack. They carried all the wounded soldiers to a nearby building which was a small grocery shop. The night before, we had placed a ten kilo TNT explosive under the shop's counter and camouflaged it with chocolate and biscuits cardboard boxes. The first enemy soldier helping himself to a treat would activate the device.

The explosion completely destroyed the building and debris blocked the road. Meanwhile, another Serbian army unit got under attack when they approached on a different route to our village.

At my position in the village center, I could see the first tanks entering the village. We were a small unit of five and had started the day in more forward positions. While we had come under direct enemy fire from tanks and 30 mm anti-aircraft guns, we had to retreat more and more. It was now the third day of the enemy's attack and I was manning a position together with a comrade. We were expecting that the enemy's main assault would happen just in front of our position. We were in a small house close to the road and the moment I entered the building, I felt that something was wrong. I couldn't put my finger on it, though, but an inner voice told me: "This place is no good!"

We waited, but nothing happened. The fighting had started on our right flank, but in front of us, everything was still calm. I told my buddy: "Let's go somewhere else!" He trusted my word and didn't argue with me and so we moved to another house that was a couple of hundred meters up the road.

On our way, we passed two of our comrades who were waiting in another position. I took a short look at their spot and told them to move fifty meters up the road to another place. I didn't know why I said it, but I somehow felt that their position was not safe. They obeyed my order and moved immediately.

Finally, the last place to go to was a big three-story house in the middle of the village. One of my comrades was upstairs under the roof with a sniper rifle and shot at the advancing enemy infantry.

All of a sudden, we had a visitor: An older soldier entered our position and said in an authoritative voice:

"I am commander XX and with the order from the brigade, I am from now in charge of this unit."

The same time he spoke his words, he was nervously eyeing out of the window as if he was afraid that the enemy would sneak up on us.

We were five guys in the room and we all looked at each other with amusement. Then one of my friends addressed the officer and told him to fuck off.

This guy was out of the door quicker than one might have guessed and we all started laughing. I think he was quite happy that he could go back to his headquarters and continue to give us his orders over the radio.

We had an M-79 OSA 90 mm RPG with us and were waiting for the enemy's tanks. Finally, a T-55 tank was approaching our positions. I fired two shots at it and it pulled back. Then another tank opened fire on our positions. We were discovered and the house we were in, provided no protection to a tank's gun.

Outside the house, bullets and shells were flying from every direction. Suddenly my alarms went off again. I stood up and said: "Let's go! Now or never!" and we all exited through a small window at the back of the house.

When I got outside the house, the air was red from the dust of the houses' red bricks. Trees were hit by artillery shells and one fell just one meter in front of my feet. I waved and screamed at the two comrades that I had left nearby and told them to join us. Somehow we all made it to a safe place.

The next day, however, the shells came in without an end and were extremely dangerous. This was easy to explain: in the beginning of their offensive, the enemy artillery had a much larger area to cover, but after several days of combat, many of our units had retreated and we were the only target left on the battlefield. All guns were directed at us. Additionally, the enemy had been able to position one or more artillery observers who were able to determine our exact location.

We were already withdrawing, not because of the artillery fire, but because we had spotted armored vehicles behind us that were threatening to cut us off. If we didn't retreat, we'd be trapped.

We had brought all our backpacks to a place in the forest a couple of days before and were on the way to pick them up when an artillery barrage surprised us.

I fell to the ground immediately and felt the earth trembling. This was not a light shaking like when a heavy truck passes in front of you, but an earthquake. We were in the middle of the forest and there was no place to hide. Branches from the trees were flying around and I was scared that

I would get pierced by a big tree branch.

There was also a lot of shrapnel. One big piece of metal landed next to my buddy. It was about ten inches (25 cm) long and was still glowing red from the heat of the explosion.

The artillery fire seemed to last forever. I remember that I was thinking that this was the type of moment when you wished you were the proverbial mouse and hide in a tiny hole.

After a while, the artillery fire moved to another place and we were able to stand up. Dust and debris fell from our uniforms, but surprisingly we were all unharmed: not a scratch!

We went to the next village which was only a mile away and once again we came under heavy artillery fire. This time, however, there were some buildings where we found cover and it was no big deal. After three weeks of heavy fighting and endless artillery fire, I was tired, exhausted, hungry and depressed: We had lost our base and things looked very bleak.

Observations

Artillery is the number one killer on the battlefield. Still, there are a few things you can do to increase your chances to survive:

Get the fuck out of the area! Artillery fire almost never starts with a couple of hundred shells coming in at the same moment. Usually, your enemy will send a few rounds, sometimes fog or smoke shells, to determine if they are on target. Only after this, do they continue with 'fire for effect' This gives you enough time to hop into a car and get as far away as possible from the danger zone.

Buildings. Better to be in the shittiest cabin than out in the open (or in a foxhole). Up to a certain caliber, a building will protect against the explosion of an artillery shell. If the building has a cellar, go there!

Disperse! Don't offer yourself as a target! Fifty infantry soldiers hanging around together are just waiting to be torn apart by artillery or airstrikes.

Keep your distance from each other: even if someone gets killed it won't be your whole unit.

Call in airstrikes/ artillery fire on your enemy! An attack is the best defense. Most modern armies have systems to quickly determine where an artillery shell was shot from and are able to strike back at their enemy's artillery positions.

Fog grenades. This will not stop the artillery from pounding you, but you will give the enemy's artillery observers a much harder job to effectively direct their fire.

Of course, when shit hits the fan, it's already too late to start thinking about how to protect yourself. Protection against artillery fire consists mainly of preventive measures and these include:

Use your instincts! If you stay in the same place for too long, in open terrain and in a position where you can be seen by the enemy, it's just a matter of time until they will call in an air or artillery strike on you. Many soldiers can 'smell' such shitty positions and avoid them.

Reinforced buildings. In Bosnia, when we had to stay in frontline cities, we would work to improve the protection on our houses. You can effectively reinforce a building with tree logs and sandbags.

Tunnels. Our enemy in Kosovo, the Serbs, brought most of their military vehicles into road or railway tunnels to protect them from NATO air strikes. This worked out very well, and they didn't lose a single vehicle that was parked in a tunnel.

Bunkers. Take the time and build some decent underground fortifications.

Camouflage. Nobody attacks you if you are not detected and seen. Don't be lazy and apply camouflage on your positions.

To direct their artillery fire, the enemy will usually have a forward observer in the area who directs their fire or, in case of an air strike, 'illuminates' the targets. There aren't that many places where such a person can be and it is often possible to either mine these spots or at least, in the event of an attack, to cover the 'suspected' places with your own fire.

Meet a Friend

When we entered the village and I looked around I saw that it was full of people. Refugees and soldiers, all of them desolate and in full retreat. I went to an empty house with my small group, found an empty room and fell asleep immediately. After an hour there was a knock on the door. When it opened I saw that it was Miguel, the Associated Press reporter who had visited us for the New Year!

He said: "Come with me!" and we went to the end of the village where his Land Rover was parked. He opened the back and there it was: A bottle of the finest Single Malt Highland Scotch Whisky!

Miguel obviously hadn't forgotten our earlier conversations. I was amazed. He must have gone to great lengths to get his hands on that bottle.

That night I shared the bottle with my comrades. For a few hours, we forgot all the chaos around us and enjoyed a good bottle in good company.

The next morning, we went back to war. We continued delaying the enemy from one village to the next. While doing this we retreated more and more into the mountains. In the end, there was no place left for us to go. We were trapped!

It was much too cold to sleep outside in the forest and while we were contemplating what to do, the artillery shelling moved away from us and so did the small arms fire. Convinced that all resistance had been broken, the enemy had sent their troops to another area.

We decided to go back to our base to deactivate our mines and booby traps. There were many civilians who were hiding out in the forest and because of the low temperatures, they were eager to return to their villages as soon as possible.

Unfortunately, for two villagers, we arrived too late. A civilian tractor with three persons on it had driven over one of our anti-tank mines and activated it. Two civilians were killed immediately while the third one was badly injured.

We learned about it from a peasant who we met on the road and who pointed us to the location. We saw a totally destroyed tractor upside down near the road, there were some blood-stained pieces of clothes around it and I found a shoe about twenty meters away from the explosion site. A farmer approached us and told us what had happened.

I wasn't too upset that one of our mines had killed some innocent civilians. Every villager knew that we had blocked the road and these guys on the tractor had obviously played with their luck. Maybe they thought that their tractor was too light to be able to activate an anti-tank mine.

Whatever their reasons were, I didn't lose much time thinking about them. It was war and people were dying all the time. Not a day went by where we didn't find a dead civilian. Most of them were killed by artillery fire, but we never did more than a superficial check to find out what had happened to them.

Less than an hour later, I forgot about the whole incident. There is always something which demanded your full attention: A booby trap on the roadside, an enemy tank convoy passing by or some guys from another unit who are giving you an update about the tactical situation.

Now that the enemy was gone, we still had to neutralize the mines at our base before more civilians got hurt.

Air Strikes!

Along with Tony, I arrived at our base in the early morning hours. The place was empty. Our mines had prevented the enemy from entering our base. It looked a little messy, but I was happy that I would be able to sleep in my own bed.

My buddy disappeared somewhere to find something to drink. While he was away, a small group of soldiers entered our base. They were from our brigade and although we weren't in the same company, we shared our quarters with them.

They were nice guys, but not the best fighters out there; I hadn't seen them during the enemy's offensive, but now that everything was clear, they were the first to reappear.

These guys seemed to be hungry. They caught a few chickens, killed them and had them in the stove in no time. I was tired and went to our office where I laid down on a couch and closed my eyes. I immediately fell into a deep sleep.

I don't know how long I had slept, but suddenly one of the soldiers shook my shoulders and screamed into my face: "Enemy infantry with tanks at two hundred meters!"

I told him to leave me the fuck alone and turned my back towards him to continue sleeping. I heard the panicky voices of our soldiers. They were leaving the base, running into the forest.

I wasn't sure what to do. There was no way, the enemy could be that close. On the other hand, it wouldn't hurt to look. I left the building and looked around me. It was already dark and I could hear some faint engine noises coming from the direction of the next village.

Those were indeed tanks! I listened for a while, but it was clear that they weren't approaching our base. Just when I finished my thoughts and relaxed a little, I saw that Tony was entering our base. He brought a crate of beer and cigarettes with him!

We sat down, drank a beer, smoked and he began to tell me what he knew about the enemy's movement. Obviously, the Serbs had left their barracks in a hurry and had started to drive all their vehicles to the countryside.

While we were pondering what our enemy was up to, we saw a bright light from far behind the mountains. Then another one to the left and then another. Many seconds later, we heard a deep rumbling sound like thunder. What we saw were gigantic explosions!

First, we thought this was some kind of super heavy artillery, but that made no sense. We had no forces in the area behind the mountains and the Serbs wouldn't shoot their own forces, would they?

Then we heard aircraft noises over our heads and everything became clear: Finally, NATO had decided to bring an end to the Serb rule over

Kosovo. They were bombing the shit out of our enemy and we were delighted!

We went inside, took our brave comrades' chickens out of the oven and started eating them all. When these guys finally realized what was going on and came back, there was nothing left for them.

Tanks!

Nobody knew at that time that the air campaign would continue for seventy-eight days. We had to keep on fighting, only that this time we had a more levelled playing field.

At night, I sometimes got outside to smoke a cigarette and then I could hear the deep rumbling sound of dozens of exploding bombs detonating miles away.

I could feel the sound in my stomach and thought: "Well, while I'm smoking my cigarette here, somebody out there is keeping our enemy busy." Then I would go back to sleep, knowing that my job had become just a little bit easier.

As long as the weather was good, the Serbs didn't dare to use their tanks. They kept them hidden from NATO in tunnels and inside bigger buildings. Without their heavy weapons, however, our enemy was rather toothless. We could deal with their infantry all the time. We called good weather 'NATO weather'.

When the weather got bad, however, they quickly deployed their tanks and started attacking.

One afternoon, my squad was fighting in the suburbs of the big city, not far away from the place where I was wounded earlier that year. I stood with one of my buddies near the road, waiting for the enemy to show up.

Suddenly, there was a very strange noise. Like a tank engine, but somehow different. I immediately started thinking: "What the fuck is this? Can't be a T-55, maybe it's one of the more lethal M-84 tanks?"

My buddy grabbed his RPG and loaded it. He removed the safety pin from the grenade and shouldered the weapon. The sound came closer, and the windows of some nearby houses started to vibrate. We became very tense, holding our breaths. Then, very slowly, around the corner a very 'strange vehicle' arrived:

A so-called 'armored tractor'. This was civilian tractor that had been converted into a makeshift armored vehicle. It was slowly crawling up the road while its totally underpowered engine made a tremendous noise and a lot of black smoke rose from the rear exhaust.

We looked at each other and started laughing. We were laughing so hard, we didn't even think about shooting it and it slowly disappeared from our field of view.

We expected a deadly fight with one of the most dangerous enemy tanks, but instead, we encountered this bundle of scrap metal from a 'Mad Max' movie.

Like on many occasions before and thereafter, laughing helped us to relieve our tensions and to remain human.

This wasn't the only time. Despite all the hardships, we laughed a lot.

A Surprising Outcome

During this time, one of my buddies had one of the strangest experiences.

A farmer showed up at our base and told us that he had fled from the fighting in his village. He said that there was still a large amount of wheat flour there and all we had to do was go to the village and pick it up. We needed all the food we could get and so we decided to check it out.

We had to wait till nightfall and then three of our soldiers took an old and battered civilian car and went on their way. They arrived near the village without any incident and parked nearby. They then carefully approached the village, unsure on whether the enemy was in the village or not.

A friend of mine took the lead. He told me later:

"In the first house, we had already found all the food that we could possibly load into the car. While my two buddies kept busy carrying all the stuff to our vehicle, I decided to take a closer look at the rest of the village.

The place was deserted and there was no living being around. When I approached the end of the village, I suddenly heard a noise. I stopped and listened: The sounds were coming from behind a big two story house. I switched my rifle to auto fire and silently walked up to the building.

I stopped and listened again: footsteps! Somebody was behind the house and was walking around it. I could discern the steps of two people. This could only be the enemy! Maybe there were more of them inside the house and these two were just outside for a smoke or to empty their bladders.

I turned to the left, walked along the wall and then carefully looked around the corner: everything was clear, but there was one more corner to go.

I paused at the next corner before I took a final look at where I thought the enemy was standing. Then I heard the footsteps again. They were moving away from me. While I was approaching them from one side, they also had started moving around, always keeping a distance from me. "Smart bastards", I thought!

Had they seen me? Were they playing cat and mouse with me or what was their plan? I decided not to follow after them, but to turn around and walk back and confront them coming my way.

I passed the two sides of the house again and stood still and listened: now the footsteps were again moving away! These fuckers had also turned around. I was pondering my situation: I was only one soldier and they were two. Maybe I should just stand still and wait for them to show up on either side.

I waited for five minutes and nothing happened. Not a sound. I started to move again and when I just had made my first step I heard the footsteps again, quickly approaching. I positioned myself at the corner of the house, rifle at the ready, staring into the dark and waiting for the enemy to come into my sights.

The footsteps slowed down. Another two or three steps and they would turn around the corner and walk straight into my gun. Sweat poured down my face.

The footsteps stopped. I could hear someone around the corner breathing, exhaling and inhaling slowly. A sudden noise and then a big shadow appeared in front of me! Instead of pulling the trigger I stumbled backwards, looked again and saw...

...a well fed and peaceful looking cow, curiously inspecting the idiot who had been sneaking around the house for the last fifteen minutes."

A short while after his encounter with the cow, we were struck by bad luck and lost a comrade.

Honor

"Despite four weeks of NATO air and missile strikes, Yugoslavia's Army and police forces have sent thousands of reinforcements into Kosovo and stepped up the use of helicopters and aircraft to press their campaign against the province's Albanians, NATO and Pentagon officials said today."

-*The New York Times,* April 20, 1999

It was a week with bad weather, which meant that the enemy's tanks were coming out of their hiding. When we got up in the morning to leave our base, we could see them already advancing on the hills around our tiny valley.

Being an easy target for the enemies' tank gunners during the day, we had to conduct all our bigger movements at night. At daytime, we only dared to operate in very small groups to defend our territory from enemy attacks.

During one of these days, the enemy attacked us from two sides and during the ensuing fight one of our comrades was killed. An artillery shell fragment pierced through his heart and he instantly died.

As it is the custom in Kosovo, we buried him the same night. There was only a small number of people present during the funeral. We didn't dare to make any light or too much noise.

When I looked around me in the moonlight I saw that just the bravest soldiers were still with us. There were also a few civilians who didn't want to leave their place and who helped us in many ways during these hard times. Although it was a sad moment, I saw an expression of pride in all the faces. It was clear to us that our comrade didn't die in vain, he died for a right cause.

There were no long speeches, just a few words and then we buried our man. I stayed with one of my buddies at the graveside and we said a last goodbye to the departed. When I saw all this brave and honest people there together, willing to sacrifice their lives, I was deeply impressed.

We had become a band of brothers.

Civilian Suffering

The more NATO bombed, the more Serbian military and paramilitary units came to our valley and occupied the empty villages. Most, if not all inhabitants had fled to the bigger cities or to Albania. The ones who stayed, however, had a very hard time.

There is no greater suffering imaginable than that of civilians in a war zone. We all know about the fate of refugees, but they are the lucky ones. They made it out of the war alive.

Many people however stay and hold out in the war zones and often nobody is there to protect them. They might have a family member who is a soldier and don't want to leave him alone.

Many of them stay because they are too old to flee or lack the financial resources to do so. Being a refugee costs a lot of money.

Once, I had the idea to take some time off from the front line, change into civilian clothes and together with a comrade, go to a nearby city and spend some time there. It was the height of the war: NATO was in the middle of their bombing campaign and the Serbs had already expelled half of the local population from their homes.

The city we went to was under Serb occupation, but most of its inhabitants were Albanians.

I have to admit that I've never been more scared in my life than during this short time as a civilian in this city. Without my gun I felt naked and helpless. I only took a hand grenade with me which I could easily conceal.

We had to sneak into the city at night as all entry points were heavily guarded by enemy checkpoints. The first thing we did in the city was to go to the part where the Albanian population was living. What I saw there reminded me of scenes in a ghetto:

Due to the enemy's ethnic cleansing campaigns in the surrounding villages this part of the city was totally overcrowded. People were camping outside everywhere. A lot of old people were there, the younger ones had already fled the country or had joined the Kosovo Liberation Army. It seemed to me that only old people, women, and kids were left.

We spent the night at the house of my comrade's sister. She was a nurse and was working a lot to help all the refugees. Her father had been beaten to death by the Serbian police a short while before. He was seventy years old when he died.

She told us to be extremely careful as there were a lot of enemy spies around and that we shouldn't trust anyone. So we decided not to walk around but spend the night at her house. There wasn't much to do outside anyway. The house was crammed with refugees from the villages, in each room were at least thirty people.

The night was uneventful, but at around five o'clock we were woken up and told to flee through a small passage at the back of the house. Serbian paramilitaries and police were raiding the street.

The Serbs didn't have any military reason to do that; they were simply going from house to house and taking money or jewelry from the inhabitants. Those who couldn't pay got beaten up, or worse.

We hurried and run down a few streets until we made a stop. There was nothing we could do to help my friend's family. We had no weapons. My comrade had an uncle at the other end of the city, far away from where we were staying, so we decided to go there.

We were not the only people fleeing: A lot of older boys and girls also left their night quarters and hit the streets. The girls afraid of getting raped and the boys of getting killed.

The problem for them was that there wasn't really a place for them to go. The city could be entered and left safely only at night. So everybody just ran to the next street corner, watched out for the Serbs and after a while ran back in the opposite direction. This was almost looking like some high school game: Dozens of people, mostly young, running to one side, stopping, turning direction and so on. But of course it was no game: They were running for their life.

We then went to my friend's uncle and spent an hour with him watching TV. All the time I was looking at a big clock hanging on the wall. I figured that the night would be relatively safe for us and I was counting the time left until nightfall.

After an hour we said goodbye and we went back to the city center. As my combat boots were torn, I went to a small shoe shop where I could repair them. Of course, I had to take the boots off while they were being fixed.

My comrade went after his own chores while I spent an hour sitting in this small shoe repair shop, in my socks, watching out of the window and hoping that no enemy patrol would enter the street and start raiding the shops and houses as they often did. I felt very pathetic in my socks and with only a hand grenade in my pocket.

Then my friend came back to pick me up and we went back to his sister's place. She gave us an account about what had happened to her:

The Serbian paramilitaries had entered her house only seconds after we had gone from there. They had asked for money and she had given them 100 Deutsche Mark, which was a lot of money. She also had to give them her wedding ring. Satisfied, they left and went to her neighbor's door. She told us that her street was targeted like this about once every week.

We ate dinner, drank tea and started swapping stories with the civilians. They were all very curious about our life on the front line. They were talking in whispers, afraid that somebody might pass by the window and overhear our conversation.

They told us about their daily terror, the beatings, and the killings. Meanwhile, I was looking at another clock on another wall and again I was counting the hours until nightfall.

My friend and I already decided that we wouldn't spend another night in the city. It was just too dangerous, not only for us, but with our presence we also endangered the whole neighborhood.

As soon as night fell we left. On our way back we saw that the Serbs had started to burn down the first houses in the city. At the end of the war, the whole city would have been burned down.

I was quite happy when we rejoined our base in the forest where I could pick up my gun and wear my uniform again. I've been totally stressed out staying in the city for only one day and one night. And these civilians were trapped there all the time! They were continuously terrorized and scared for their life while their living conditions were beyond horrible.

I thought, and still do, that as soldiers we had a much easier plight then these civilians. At least we could face the enemy in a battle and fight back.

The civilians in the city were completely powerless. They never knew what would happen next and nobody was there to protect them.

Observations

From Sarajevo to Aleppo, it is always the civilian population that suffers the most in every armed conflict. Here are the dos and the don'ts when it comes to surviving the war as a civilian.

First of all, don't think that you can survive a war by hiding in your basement with a two year supply of food and water. You have to be mobile. If the war comes to your hometown, then flee! The further you are away from the fighting, the better. If you are sitting on thousands of dollars' worth of survival meals in the basement of your cozy home, you'll probably make the wrong decision and want to stay.

Go to the big cities! The more people around you the better the chances of surviving. Many people means many witnesses. Enemy soldiers and criminal gangs are less inclined to kill you just for the fun of it.

If you stay in the countryside, you'll be fair game for everybody: Marauding soldiers, criminals, and militias will make your life a living hell, even if there is no fighting going on.

Don't take a gun with you! People will perceive you as a threat and while criminals will more likely kill you than without a gun, the enemy will execute you for being an irregular insurgent or terrorist.

Cash is King. Put your cash in a condom and then hide it in your rectum. Not all of it, though. You don't want to pull it out of there every time you have to pay for something.

Take some cigarettes with you, even if you don't smoke. Sharing a smoke with an enemy soldier at a checkpoint or a crook who is thinking about robbing you diffuses the situation.

Cigarettes, antibiotics, and morphine are alternative currencies in many wars. While your cash might become worthless, the value of these three items grow the longer the war goes on. Morphine especially would be highly demanded as there will be lots of wounded people, but also many drug addicts who will swap their food in exchange for the drug.

Don't wear fancy stuff. Leave your expensive clothes at home and dress something simple. You don't want to get noticed, so don't dress in bright colors. But also don't wear any military clothes or camouflage as you might be mistaken for a soldier.

You will have to walk a lot, so get yourself a comfortable pair of shoes.

Information is very important. Take a cheap shortwave radio with you to find out where the front lines are and where food and shelter can be found. If refugee camps have been set up, then go there. The living conditions in these camps are often horrible, but they'll offer you security.

You might get separated from your family or friends. Designate places where you can reunite with them or where you can leave messages for each other.

Every war is different and a lot of things that you have to do depend on the situation. For example, you might also want to take things like maps, torches or a first-aid kit with you.

In the end, what will be much more important than any physical item that can be carried around will be your mindset: The willingness to leave everything behind, to swallow your pride, to hide your feelings and to carry on.

Helping People

The longer the war went on, the more the Serbs were moving their troops to the countryside. Soon, all villages around our base were occupied by the enemy.

A friend of mine lived in a village a couple of miles away from our base. He was a KLA guerrilla fighter like we were, but not in our unit. From time to time, he came to our base to help us and this is how we knew each other.

One afternoon, he called us over the radio and asked if anyone wanted to go to his village. There were some problems with the enemy, he stated.

I thought "why not?" and left with a group of soldiers. On our way to the village, we got updates on the situation there. There was bad news and two of the soldiers in our group stopped and said they didn't want to continue.

There was nothing we could do as this was purely a voluntary mission and we had no orders from anyone to go there. We continued our way without them.

We came to a wooded hill where we could see our friend's place; it was situated on another hill and all we had to do was to cross a small valley to get there.

When we descended into the valley, we left another soldier behind. We were only two now and I was leading. When I came out of the woods into the open, I could see our friend at the entry of the village. He waved at us.

I saw that there were plenty of other soldiers higher up on the village's main street and started wondering: "Why is he calling us for help when there are plenty of his own soldiers around?"

I got an answer very quickly. I was now only 200 meters away from the first houses when a bullet zipped over my head. Then another one and then many more.

A machine gun was taking aim at us. We stopped, and ran back. We were completely in the open and there was no cover in either direction. While I ran, hundreds of more bullets were coming in my direction.

It dawned on me: The other soldiers I had seen in the village were the enemy! Unable to fight them off alone, my friend had gone into hiding and had called us for help. His waving at me had been a way to get my attention and to warn me! I had misunderstood the whole situation.

There was at least a complete infantry company of Serbs in the village and more and more of them started shooting at us.

I saw a small manure pile and hid behind it. This wasn't the best cover, but there was absolutely nothing else out there.

While I laid flat on the ground the bullets kept flying towards me. They must have had a lot of ammunition! I heard how the bullets struck the manure pile and I just hoped that it was thick enough to protect me.

I looked at the grass in front of my eyes and I literally wished I was a mouse and could just hide in a tiny hole in the ground.

Meanwhile, the other soldier who had come with me made it to safety. He had run a little faster and had reached the woods of the hill. He was calling me, but I didn't dare to move.

I was waiting for a break in the enemy's fire to make a jump for cover. After what seemed like an eternity to me, but was maybe only a minute, I stood up and raced towards the woods.

Bullets were everywhere and I heard dozens of nasty 'zip' sounds while I crashed into the underbrush. There was a very low stone wall where my buddy was hiding. We were safe, but we still had to wait for another five minutes until the enemy ceased fire.

Miraculously, we were unharmed. I lost my 'Bugs Bunny' baseball cap which I had gotten as a present from some kids just a few days ago, but that was all.

The next days, I wondered a lot about the fate of the friend we had seen in his village. Did he make it out alive?

I saw him a week later when he came to our base as if nothing had happened. He thanked me for my goodwill on that day and told everyone: "I called you all for help, but the only person who came to my assistance was the German!"

I was thinking: "Yeah, but the German only came, because he didn't know what was going on." Instead, I smiled and said: "Anytime!"

Time for a Bath!

Sometimes we would even 'share' the village we occupied with our enemy:

There was a mountain crest separating our base from the enemy's villages and therefore we were not overly concerned about their presence (they had no direct line of fire). Still, we would climb the mountains from time to time and descend to their village to keep an eye on them.

This was one big village with many houses. There were not enough enemy forces to occupy the whole place, let alone organize a defense perimeter.

On one occasion, we approached an occupied house. This was more or less a reconnaissance mission without a concrete plan. We just went there to see if the enemy was still there, what they were doing and maybe catch a chicken or two on our way back to bring them to our base.

While we were observing the enemy, I looked around to see if all of my comrades were still with me. One was missing. I asked the soldier next to me where the guy might be and he just pointed in one direction with his finger.

Our man had gone to an empty farmhouse which was very close to the enemy. He had lit a fire in the kitchen stove to heat up some water which he poured into a big metal bucket. Now, with the help of another soldier, he carried the bucket outside to the house's porch. Without the slightest care in the world, he undressed completely and disappeared into his improvised bathtub. As he was a small boy, he nicely fit into the giant bucket.

I was speechless. This was either the dumbest or the coolest thing I'd ever seen a soldier doing. It was too late to stop our man anyway, so we decided to just watch him and, in case the enemy became aware of his presence, provide him with covering fire.

The enemy didn't move. They must have seen the smoke from the chimney, but either they thought that it was one of their own who started the fire or they were just as surprised as I was. Either way, after our comrade had finished his bath we went back to our base, five sweaty and stinking soldiers and a fresh-smelling, pink-skinned and smiling one.

The Endgame

Some days later, the Serbs amassed a lot of infantry, put them on trucks and came to our village. One of our observers counted thirty trucks. That meant at least two enemy infantry companies against our two remaining squads. We were used to being outnumbered, but this time there were simply too many. Our logistics and support units and half of our platoon had already left our base and had gone deeper into the mountains.

We finally decided to join them. They had already called us several times over the radio, fearing that we might get caught or killed by the enemy. To reach them meant that we had to walk one day and one night, mostly through a rough terrain and some territories that might be under enemy control.

We planned to return as soon as possible, so there was no need to carry all our gear with us. I put out a poncho liner and we made two piles: A big one with the stuff that we would leave behind (rifle grenades, hand grenades, explosives) and a very small one with the few items we would take along with us (two AK-47 assault rifles with spare mags and two water bottles).

On our way through the forest, we encountered another group of KLA soldiers who went the same direction and we joined them. They knew the directions and being in a bigger group gave us some protection. Unfortunately, none of them had any smokes left.

We marched the whole night, uphill and in rough terrain. It was the beginning of June and quite hot, even at night, and lack of water started to become a problem. There was nothing to do, except reach our mountain refuge as soon as possible.

Finally, in the early morning hours, we arrived at our destination. Under the foliage of a dense forest, there was a complete improvised city. Hundreds of people who lived under big plastic sheets. They had just woken up and started very small campfires. The small smoke piles were dispersed by the forest's canopy and couldn't be detected by enemy artillery observers. There were tents for everything: A command tent, guard tents, a kitchen and a bakery tent. Most tents, however, were occupied by civilian refugees. Kids were running around everywhere and I somehow envied them. They didn't grasp the seriousness of the situation and played happily just like they would in peacetime.

I soon learned a few disturbing things:

Food was scarce. Due to the high number of refugees, there was simply not enough to eat for everybody. There were long queues of people waiting at the kitchen tent and some of them were openly showing their discontent for having to wait hours for a small cup of watery soup. The parole was: "Soldiers eat first" and although nobody openly complained about it, I'm sure that some people weren't too pleased about it. Some local farmers had given tons of wheat, potatoes, cabbage or beans to the Kosovo Liberation Army since the beginning of the conflict and now they had to wait in line to get a tiny clump of bread.

The other problem was the enemy. It turned out that there was a village about a kilometer downhill from the camp. It was under KLA control, but during the last days, it had been repeatedly shelled by the enemy's artillery. Some shells had even landed near the camp in the forest. Should the Serbs decide to attack this village they would undoubtedly discover the camp and this would mean a total disaster. The whole idea behind setting up the camp in the mountains was its stealth, nobody thought about how to defend it.

I already started to curse my decision to come up here. We asked our way through to our unit and finally found them: they had descended into the nearby village and had occupied a small house near the enemy's positions. This way they didn't have to see the chaos and bickering in the camp, but had to deal with an occasional artillery attack.

We were happy to see them. While my friend reported about our time in the village, I was offered a cup of Turkish coffee and- a cigarette! I slowly inhaled the smoke and enjoyed it enormously. Everybody was fine, even the lightly wounded soldiers who had decided to stay with our unit instead of giving themselves into the care of a KLA field hospital. There was a lot of talk about what we should do. All of us were battle experienced fighters and every opinion had the same weight. The times when commanders had given us orders were long gone.

I decided to go back to where we came from. I spoke with my buddy and he immediately agreed to go with me. Another three guys from the unit decided to join us, too. I was pleased: These guys were the best soldiers of our unit and also only a small group, we were a force to reckon with. As there was nothing to gain from staying in the mountains we left immediately.

We bid our farewells and started the long way back. This time we descended the mountains and everything was much easier. Although we had no idea what the future was holding for us, we went back to a place that we intimately knew and where we had fought numerous times. We had our weapons, enough ammo and there were hidden food stocks all around the village. We could make it on our own.

We marched the whole day and arrived at our old base in record time. Just before nightfall, we reached the edge of the forest from where we had a first view of our village.

Suddenly, we heard some truck noises in the village, but we couldn't make out if these trucks were coming or going or how many trucks there were.

I decided to check it out. We had a machine gunner in our group and the two of us went down to the village on a recce patrol. It was now almost night and as we couldn't see much we stopped every ten meters and listened for a while if we could detect any suspicious noise. This was a very slow procedure but we had no idea what to expect and if there were enemy troops in the village, we didn't want to alarm them.

As we approached the center of the village, our machine gunner touched my arm. I stopped immediately.

He whispered: "I think I heard something!"

We stood and listened. I didn't hear anything suspicious, just the faint evening breeze.

I said: "You're sure?"

He: "I think someone's talking."

Me: "Albanian or Serbian?"

He: "Dunno."

We listened for another minute.

He:" What we do?"

Me: "I don't know."

With my finger on the trigger of my AK-47, I started to walk further down the road. It was now almost completely dark and I thought it was worth the risk. My buddy followed me. We passed the burnt out village school and then another building which was still intact. I decided to go inside and check it out. We could take a short break there and then continue our mission. The building was on our right-hand side and its door was open. I was just about to enter it when a man quickly moved out of the door and turned to the right. In the dark, he didn't notice us and moved away. I saw the silhouette of an assault rifle in his hands. Suddenly, he froze and started to turn around...

I opened fire. Two short bursts from my Kalashnikov. I swiftly ducked away to the left and my comrade opened fire with his machine gun. This was a rehearsed maneuver: Every time we made enemy contact, the point man (the first man) would shoot and the rest of the team would spread out to get a clean line of fire. The machine gunner would stay in the middle and just fire away.

My buddy shot about fifty bullets before I told him to cease fire. We retreated immediately. It turned out that the building I was about to enter was occupied by a platoon of Serbian paramilitaries! The trucks we had heard before had brought them there.

Now all hell broke loose! After the initial surprise, the enemy quickly figured out that they were under attack and started firing in our direction. Luckily, it was night and we could make it safely to the edge of the forest where the rest of our group was waiting. They almost mistook us for Serbs and when I ran into the first guy his eyes were wide open and he said: "You assholes, I almost killed you! I thought you were Serbs!"

I led our group to the place where I had slept two nights before. We were all exhausted and fell asleep. The next morning we split into two teams and started to reconnoiter the area. My friend and I decided to take the guy with the machine gun with us, while the two soldiers of our second team had a multiple grenade launcher and an RPG. We would meet them every three or four hours to share information.

It turned out that there was a heavy enemy presence in the village. We identified four more buildings occupied by paramilitaries, one with a mortar position. There was a fifth fortified position on a hill at the opposite side of the village from where the enemy had a very good look at the whole valley.

We were five guys with a machine gun, an RPG, a multiple grenade launcher and a lot of rifle grenades. In the afternoon we met another three KLA soldiers from our brigade. They had been hiding out in the forest the whole time, but had heard the firefight of the last evening. Knowing that there must be more KLA units in the valley they came out of the forest and spotted our second team. This was good news. These three guys were very experienced soldiers and knew the village very well.

Even better, one of them carried a light RPD machine gun and they also had a couple of car batteries hidden in a barn which we could use to charge our radio batteries. They also knew the whereabouts of a lot of food stashes. We were now three teams of combat experienced guerrilla fighters. Not bad at all.

As our little war council went on, we heard a truck coming up the road. It drove towards the paramilitaries near the school. Either they must have thought that we were all gone or maybe the enemy hadn't yet informed their logistics that they had been under attack the last night.

There was no time for us to set up a proper ambush, but we were able to damage the truck when it parked near the school to supply the paramilitaries. They shot back at us, but as they didn't know our exact locations, all their bullets missed.

During the next few days, we attacked three more enemy positions and one enemy patrol. The most memorable of these attacks was executed by our team three. One of their soldiers reported to us:

"We went straight into the center of the village. We only took the small alleyways which are flanked by high walls on both sides. As we passed one of these walls, we heard some noises from the other side. One of my comrades helped me to take a look over the wall and what I saw surprised me:

Two Serbian paramilitaries lying on the ground, bare chested and obviously sunbathing! We couldn't use our light machine gun as there was no way to properly aim over the wall without making noise. So I took out my pistol and shot both of them, while my two comrades were holding my feet to lift me high enough over the wall. Then we threw a hand grenade over the wall and quickly made our way out of the village."

There were a lot of weapons in the village, hidden by the KLA, which we now 'unearthed': We added a 14.5 mm heavy machine gun and a 12.7 mm Barrett sniper rifle to our arsenal.

Our small war tactics proved to be extremely successful. The enemy was completely confused and suffered many casualties while only one of our own fighters suffered a light flesh wound from a bullet.

After three days of fighting, the enemy decided they had enough and left town. We watched them packing their stuff and setting the few remaining houses on fire. Then they hastily mounted their trucks and were gone. The war would last another two days before the Serbs officially withdrew all their troops from Kosovo.

Another war was over!

Afterword

Fortunately, most of the persons depicted in these stories are still alive. Pierre, my friend from Bosnia, now lives in Croatia and works as a private drone operator. Stefano, the Italian volunteer, is married to a Croatian woman and has several children. They live in Mostar.

Blerim, who set up our unit in Kosovo, has become a successful businessman, while Naim, the 'rabbit', is still a soldier. He and Tony serve together in the Kosovo Security Forces.

Sadly, Miguel, the AP reporter died. A couple of days after the war ended, he came to see us in our new base in a recently liberated city. We had a couple of drinks and started swapping stories about what happened to each other since we last met.

Later on, he went to cover the war in Chechnya, but he came back for a short visit to Kosovo where we met again. In 2000 Miguel was killed in an ambush while covering the civil war in Sierra Leone.

We miss him.

821.112.2-94

Bartetzko, Roland

The Smell of War : lessons from the
Battlefield / Roland Bartetzko. - Prishtinë :
SMS, 2017. – 134 f. ; 21 cm.

ISBN 978-9951-562-35-5

Made in the USA
Middletown, DE
04 January 2021